Horizons

Mathematics

K

Book 2
Lessons 81–160

Author:

Alan Christopherson, M.S.

Graphic Design:

Jennifer Davis

Editorial/Illustration:

Kyle Bennett   *Karen Eubanks*
Theresa Buskey   *Keith Piccolo*
JoAnn Cumming   *Brian Ring*
Chris Burkholder   *Dawn Tessier*
Lauren Durain   *Annette Walker*

Alpha Omega Publications, Inc. • Rock Rapids, IA

Horizons Mathematics K, Book 2
© MM by Alpha Omega Publications, Inc. All rights reserved.
804 N. 2nd Ave. E., Rock Rapids, IA 51246-1759

Printed in the United States of America
ISBN 978-0-7403-0310-4

Lesson 81

1 Write the number before.

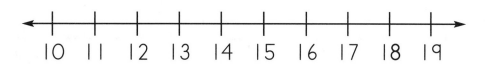

10 11 12 13 14 15 16 17 18 19

____ 12	____ 15	____ 14
____ 18	____ 19	____ 11
____ 16	____ 13	____ 17

2 Circle the greater number in each pair.

| 12   6 | 4   7 | 18   11 |
| 5   8 | 13   19 | 15   2 |

3 Circle the smaller number of each pair.

13 7	5 8	19 12

6 9	12 18	16 3

4 Add.

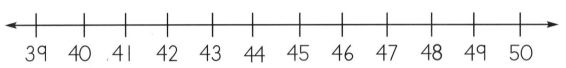

39 40 41 42 43 44 45 46 47 48 49 50

```
  44        48        41        43        49
+  1      +  1      +   3     +   2     +   1
____      ____      _____     _____     _____
```

```
  39        42        45        46        48
+  1      +   4     +   3     +   1     +   2
____      _____     _____     _____     _____
```

```
  40        47        44        41        50
+   3     +   2     +   2     +   4     +   0
_____     _____     _____     _____     _____
```

Horizons Math K Book 2

Lesson 82

1 Write the number after.

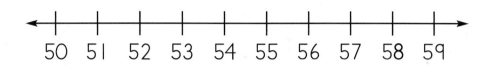

| 56 ____ | 51 ____ | 54 ____ |

| 58 ____ | 55 ____ | 50 ____ |

| 52 ____ | 57 ____ | 53 ____ |

2 Write the number before.

| ____ 19 | ____ 14 | ____ 12 |

| ____ 17 | ____ 16 | ____ 18 |

| ____ 11 | ____ 15 | ____ 13 |

 Add.

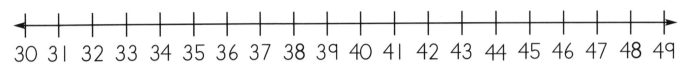

30 31 32 33 34 35 36 37 38 39 40 41 42 43 44 45 46 47 48 49

32	44	41	35
+ 1	+ 4	+ 3	+ 4

39	46	42	33
+ 1	+ 3	+ 1	+ 2

© MM.....

30	40	43	37
+ 2	+ 0	+ 2	+ 1

④ Circle the smaller number in each pair.

11 8	13 15	1 4

7 6	16 17	9 5

Lesson 83

1

JANUARY						
Sun	Mon	Tues	Wed	Thurs	Fri	Sat
			1	2	3	4
5	6	7	8	9	10	11
12	13	14	15	16	17	18
19	20	21	22	23	24	25
26	27	28	29	30	31	

FEBRUARY						
Sun	Mon	Tues	Wed	Thurs	Fri	Sat
						1
2	3	4	5	6	7	8
9	10	11	12	13	14	15
16	17	18	19	20	21	22
23	24	25	26	27	28	

MARCH						
Sun	Mon	Tues	Wed	Thurs	Fri	Sat
						1
2	3	4	5	6	7	8
9	10	11	12	13	14	15
16	17	18	19	20	21	22
23/30	24/31	25	26	27	28	29

APRIL						
Sun	Mon	Tues	Wed	Thurs	Fri	Sat
		1	2	3	4	5
6	7	8	9	10	11	12
13	14	15	16	17	18	19
20	21	22	23	24	25	26
27	28	29	30			

MAY						
Sun	Mon	Tues	Wed	Thurs	Fri	Sat
				1	2	3
4	5	6	7	8	9	10
11	12	13	14	15	16	17
18	19	20	21	22	23	24
25	26	27	28	29	30	31

JUNE						
Sun	Mon	Tues	Wed	Thurs	Fri	Sat
1	2	3	4	5	6	7
8	9	10	11	12	13	14
15	16	17	18	19	20	21
22	23	24	25	26	27	28
29	30					

JULY						
Sun	Mon	Tues	Wed	Thurs	Fri	Sat
		1	2	3	4	5
6	7	8	9	10	11	12
13	14	15	16	17	18	19
20	21	22	23	24	25	26
27	28	29	30	31		

AUGUST						
Sun	Mon	Tues	Wed	Thurs	Fri	Sat
					1	2
3	4	5	6	7	8	9
10	11	12	13	14	15	16
17	18	19	20	21	22	23
24/31	25	26	27	28	29	30

SEPTEMBER						
Sun	Mon	Tues	Wed	Thurs	Fri	Sat
	1	2	3	4	5	6
7	8	9	10	11	12	13
14	15	16	17	18	19	20
21	22	23	24	25	26	27
28	29	30				

OCTOBER						
Sun	Mon	Tues	Wed	Thurs	Fri	Sat
			1	2	3	4
5	6	7	8	9	10	11
12	13	14	15	16	17	18
19	20	21	22	23	24	25
26	27	28	29	30	31	

NOVEMBER						
Sun	Mon	Tues	Wed	Thurs	Fri	Sat
						1
2	3	4	5	6	7	8
9	10	11	12	13	14	15
16	17	18	19	20	21	22
23/30	24	25	26	27	28	29

DECEMBER						
Sun	Mon	Tues	Wed	Thurs	Fri	Sat
	1	2	3	4	5	6
7	8	9	10	11	12	13
14	15	16	17	18	19	20
21	22	23	24	25	26	27
28	29	30	31			

How many days are in a week? _____

How many months are in a year? _____

How many months have 30 days? _____

How many months have 31 days? _____

Horizons Math K Book 2

2 Write the number after.

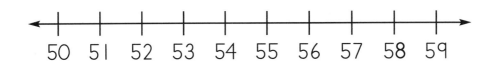

50 51 52 53 54 55 56 57 58 59

52 _____	55 _____	51 _____
57 _____	54 _____	50 _____
58 _____	53 _____	56 _____

3 Write the number before.

10 11 12 13 14 15 16 17 18 19

_____ 15	_____ 11	_____ 16
_____ 12	_____ 17	_____ 13
_____ 18	_____ 14	_____ 19

Lesson 84

1 Count by 2's.

1		3		5		7		9	
11		13		15		17		19	
21		23		25		27		29	
31		33		35		37		39	
41		43		45		47		49	
51		53		55		57		59	
61		63		65		67		69	
71		73		75		77		79	

2 Add.

50 51 52 53 54 55 56 57 58 59

50 + 1 = _____   55 + 2 = _____

52 + 0 = _____   58 + 1 = _____

56 + 0 = _____   57 + 1 = _____

51 + 2 = _____   54 + 1 = _____

3 There are _____ months in a year.

January	February	March	April
May	June	July	August
September	October	November	December

1. Write the last month of the year. _____

2. Write the first month of the year. _____

3. Write the month that it is now. _____

4 Count the money.

    _____ ¢

   ¢

  _____ ¢

 _____ ¢

Horizons Math K Book 2

Lesson 85

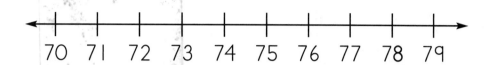

1 Write the number between.

70 71 72 73 74 75 76 77 78 79

72 ____ 74	77 ____ 79	70 ____ 72
71 ____ 73	76 ____ 78	73 ____ 75
70 ____ 72	75 ____ 77	74 ____ 76

2 Count by 2's.

2		6		10		14		18	
	24		28		32		36		40
42		46		50		54		58	
	64		68		72		76		80

3 How many months are in a year? _____

How many days are in a week? _____

4 Add.

50 51 52 53 54 55 56 57 58 59

```
  50        50        56        54
+  3      +  1      +  0      +  1
```

```
  58        52        51        57
+  1      +  2      +  3      +  1
```

```
  53        55        59        52
+  2      +  1      +  0      +  3
```

Horizons Math K Book 2

Lesson 86

1 Count by 2's.

	2		4		6		8		10
	12		14		16		18		20
	22		24		26		28		30
	32		34		36		38		40
	42		44		46		48		50
	52		54		56		58		60
	62		64		66		68		70
	72		74		76		78		80

2 Add.

50 51 52 53 54 55 56 57 58 59

```
  52        56        54        50
+  2      +  3      +  4      +  3
```

```
  55        53        52        57
+  3      +  2      +  3      +  2
```

3 Count by 2's.

2		6		10		14		18	
	24		28		32		36		40
42		46		50		54		58	
	64		68		72		76		80

4 Write the number between.

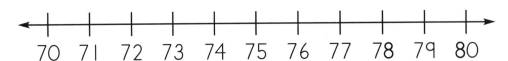

70 71 72 73 74 75 76 77 78 79 80

| 71 _____ 73 | 77 _____ 79 | 70 _____ 72 |
| 74 _____ 76 | 78 _____ 80 | 73 _____ 75 |

Lesson 87

1 Write the number **before**.

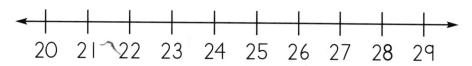

20 21 22 23 24 25 26 27 28 29

_____ 22	_____ 25	_____ 24
_____ 28	_____ 29	_____ 21
_____ 26	_____ 23	_____ 27

2 Circle the **odd** numbers.

1	2	3	4	5	6	7	8	9	10
11	12	13	14	15	16	17	18	19	20
21	22	23	24	25	26	27	28	29	30
31	32	33	34	35	36	37	38	39	40
41	42	43	44	45	46	47	48	49	50
51	52	53	54	55	56	57	58	59	60
61	62	63	64	65	66	67	68	69	70
71	72	73	74	75	76	77	78	79	80

3 Find the perimeter.

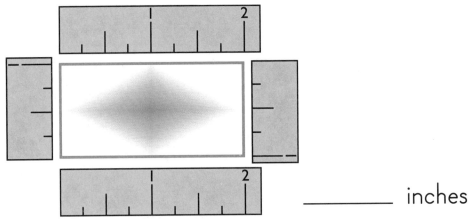

_____ inches

4 Count the money.

 _ _ _ _ _ _ _ _ ¢

  _ _ _ _ _ _ _ _ ¢

 _ _ _ _ _ _ _ _ ¢

  _ _ _ _ _ _ _ _ ¢

5 Add.

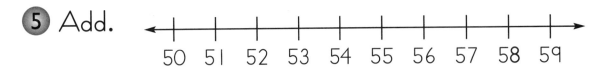

50 51 52 53 54 55 56 57 58 59

57 + 2 = _____   54 + 3 = _____

50 + 4 = _____   55 + 4 = _____

52 + 3 = _____   56 + 2 = _____

Horizons Math K Book 2

Lesson 88

① Write the number after.

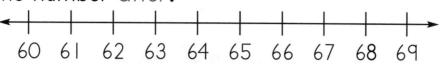
60 61 62 63 64 65 66 67 68 69

66 _____	61 _____	64 _____
68 _____	65 _____	60 _____
62 _____	67 _____	63 _____

② Write the number before.

20 21 22 23 24 25 26 27 28 29

_____ 29	_____ 24	_____ 22
_____ 27	_____ 26	_____ 28
_____ 21	_____ 25	_____ 23

③ Write the missing odd numbers.

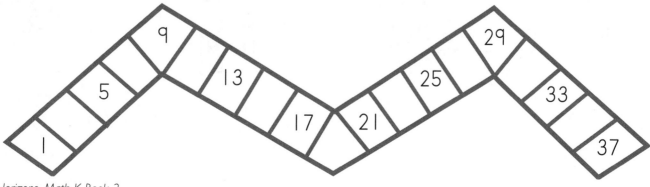

© MM, Alpha Omega Publications, Inc.

4 Find the perimeter.

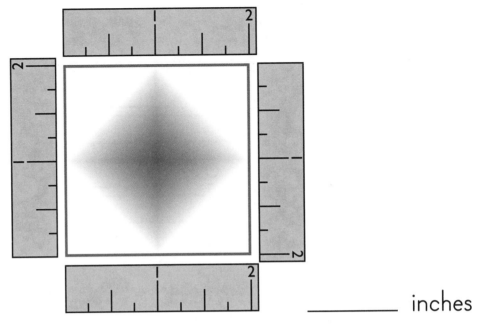

_____ inches

5 Add.

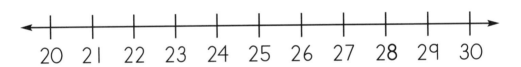

27 + 2	20 + 4	23 + 3	26 + 2

21 + 4	25 + 3	22 + 4	28 + 2

Lesson 89

① Write the time in the blanks.

11:00

The time is _____ o'clock.

One hour before is _____ o'clock.

One hour after is _____ o'clock.

The time is _____ o'clock.

One hour before is _____ o'clock.

One hour after is _____ o'clock.

The time is _____ o'clock.

One hour before is _____ o'clock.

One hour after is _____ o'clock.

The time is _____ o'clock.

One hour before is _____ o'clock.

One hour after is _____ o'clock.

2 Write the number after.

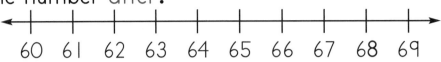

60 61 62 63 64 65 66 67 68 69

62 _____	65 _____	61 _____
67 _____	64 _____	60 _____
68 _____	63 _____	66 _____

3 Write the number before.

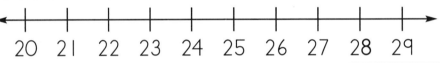

20 21 22 23 24 25 26 27 28 29

_____ 21	_____ 26	_____ 22
_____ 25	_____ 23	_____ 28
_____ 29	_____ 27	_____ 24

4 Write the missing even numbers.

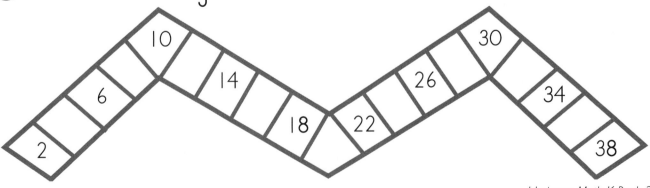

© MM, Alpha Omega Publications, Inc.

Horizons Math K Book 2

Lesson 90

1 Count to 90.

¢ ¢ ¢ ¢ ¢ ¢ ¢ ¢ ¢ ¢
¢ ¢ ¢ ¢ ¢ ¢ ¢ ¢ ¢ ¢
¢ ¢ ¢ ¢ ¢ ¢ ¢ ¢ ¢ ¢
¢ ¢ ¢ ¢ ¢ ¢ ¢ ¢ ¢ ¢
¢ ¢ ¢ ¢ ¢ ¢ ¢ ¢ ¢ ¢
¢ ¢ ¢ ¢ ¢ ¢ ¢ ¢ ¢ ¢
¢ ¢ ¢ ¢ ¢ ¢ ¢ ¢ ¢ ¢
¢ ¢ ¢ ¢ ¢ ¢ ¢ ¢ ¢ ¢
¢ ¢ ¢ ¢ ¢ ¢ ¢ ¢ ¢ ¢

2 Write the time in the blanks.

6:00

The time is _____ o'clock.
One hour before is _____ o'clock.
One hour after is _____ o'clock.

The time is _____ o'clock.
One hour before is _____ o'clock.
One hour after is _____ o'clock.

The time is _____ o'clock.
One hour before is _____ o'clock.
One hour after is _____ o'clock.

The time is _____ o'clock.
One hour before is _____ o'clock.
One hour after is _____ o'clock.

3 Write the number after.

60 ____	65 ____	61 ____
66 ____	62 ____	67 ____
63 ____	68 ____	64 ____
69 ____	44 ____	52 ____

4 Write the number before.

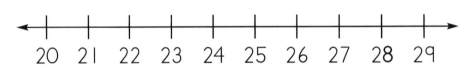

```
←——+——+——+——+——+——+——+——+——+——+——→
   20  21  22  23  24  25  26  27  28  29
```

____ 25	____ 29	____ 24
____ 28	____ 23	____ 27
____ 22	____ 26	____ 21

help!

© MM, Alpha Omega Publications, Inc.

Horizons Math K Book 2

Lesson 91

① Add.

60 61 62 63 64 65 66 67 68 69

```
  60
+  1
────
```

```
  65
+  2
────
```

```
  62
+  0
────
```

```
  68
+  1
────
```

```
  66
+  0
────
```

```
  67
+  1
────
```

```
  61
+  2
────
```

```
  64
+  1
────
```

② How many months are in a year? _____

What is the third month in a year? _____

In which month is your birthday? _____

What month is it today? _____

3 Add.

30 31 32 33 34 35 36 37 38 39 40

32 + 4 = _____   36 + 4 = _____

30 + 5 = _____   34 + 3 = _____

33 + 6 = _____   35 + 3 = _____

37 + 3 = _____   38 + 2 = _____

© MM, Alpha Omega Publications, Inc.

4 How many inches?

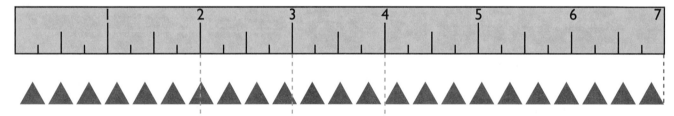

 _____ inches

 _____ inches

 _____ inches

 _____ inches

Lesson 92

1 Count the volume.

This is a quart.   This is a gallon.

This is a liter.   This is a cup.

    _____ quarts

 _____ gallons

   _____ liters

  _____ cups

2 Add.

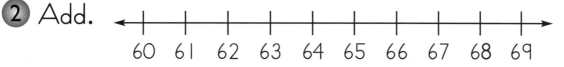

60 + 3 = _____   60 + 1 = _____   66 + 0 = _____

64 + 1 = _____   68 + 1 = _____   62 + 2 = _____

61 + 3 = _____   67 + 1 = _____   63 + 2 = _____

65 + 1 = _____   69 + 0 = _____   62 + 3 = _____

3 Count by 2's.

2			8			14			20			26		
32			38			44			50			56		
62			68			74			80			86		

4 Add.

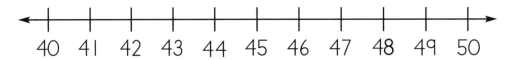

```
  48          47          45          43
+  2        +  3        +  3        +  4
```

```
  44          40          46          42
+  3        +  5        +  4        +  5
```

```
  41          43          49          50
+  7        +  6        +  1        +  0
```

© MM, Alpha Omega Publications, Inc.

Lesson 93

_____

1 Write the number **after**.

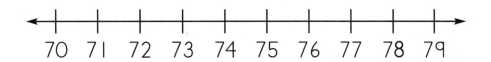

70	71	72	73	74	75	76	77	78	79

70 _____   73 _____   71 _____

78 _____   76 _____   77 _____

75 _____   72 _____   74 _____

2 Count the volumes.

 _____ quarts

 _____ cups

 _____ gallons

 _____ liters

3 Add the money.

    +   = _____ ¢

 +   = _____ ¢

  +   = _____ ¢

 +   = _____ ¢

4 Add.

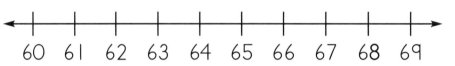

```
  67        65        62        68
+  2      +  3      +  4      +  1
```

```
  66        60        61        64
+  0      +  3      +  6      +  3
```

```
  63        65        67        60
+  4      +  0      +  1      +  0
```

Lesson 94

1 Write the number between.

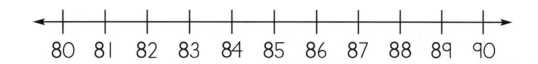

85 ____ 87	81 ____ 83	88 ____ 90
80 ____ 82	86 ____ 88	84 ____ 86
87 ____ 89	82 ____ 84	83 ____ 85

2 Count the volumes.

 _____ cups

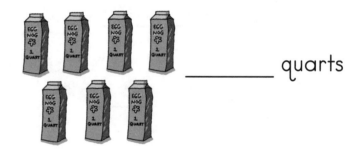 _____ quarts

 _____ liters

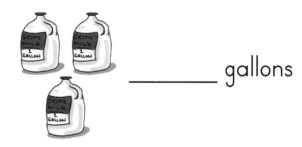 _____ gallons

3 Write the number after.

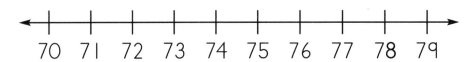

70 71 72 73 74 75 76 77 78 79

71 ____	72 ____	73 ____
74 ____	75 ____	7 6 ____
77 ____	78 ____	70 ____

4 Add.

60 61 62 63 64 65 66 67 68 69 70

63 + 4 = _____   60 + 5 = _____

67 + 3 = _____   62 + 4 = _____

68 + 2 = _____   61 + 5 = _____

66 + 3 = _____   63 + 2 = _____

61 + 7 = _____   60 + 6 = _____

Horizons Math K Book 2

Lesson 95

place value

tens | ones

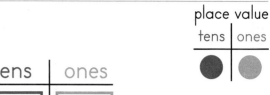

1 Write the numbers.

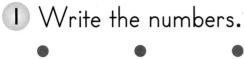

 tens | ones

$=$ _____

 tens | ones

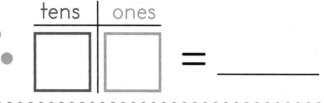

$=$ _____

 tens | ones

$=$ _____

 tens | ones

$=$ _____

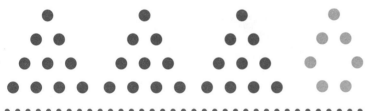 tens | ones

$=$ _____

 tens | ones

$=$ _____

© MM, Alpha Omega Publications, Inc.

Horizons Math K Book 2

2 Write the number between.

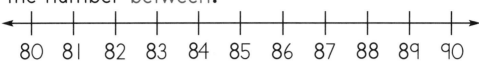

88 _____ 90	80 _____ 82	87 _____ 89
81 _____ 83	86 _____ 88	82 _____ 84
85 _____ 87	83 _____ 85	85 _____ 87

3 Count the volumes.

 _____ liters

 _____ cups

 _____ quarts

 _____ gallons

4 Write the number after.

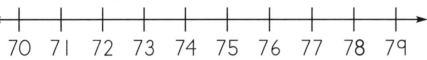

78 _____	72 _____	77 _____
74 _____	76 _____	71 _____
73 _____	70 _____	75 _____

Lesson 96

1 Add.

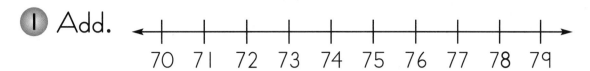

70 71 72 73 74 75 76 77 78 79

```
  75          76          74          77
+  2        +  0        +  4        +  2
```

```
  71          78          70          79
+  2        +  0        +  1        +  0
```

```
  72          76          78          70
+  4        +  3        +  1        +  2
```

2 Write the numbers.

place value
tens | ones

  tens | ones = _____

tens | ones = _____

 tens | ones = _____

3 Fill in the odd numbers.

1			7		13		19		25		
31		37		43		49		55			
61		67		73		79		85			

4 Add.

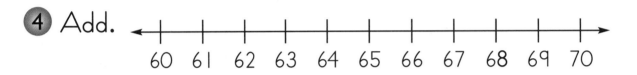

60 61 62 63 64 65 66 67 68 69 70

```
  62        67        61        66
+  5      +  3      +  6      +  3
```

```
  60        68        61        60
+  5      +  2      +  7      +  4
```

Lesson 97

1 Write the number after.

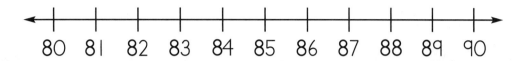

80 81 82 83 84 85 86 87 88 89 90

81 _____	84 _____	88 _____
85 _____	82 _____	87 _____
80 _____	86 _____	83 _____

2 Add.

70 71 72 73 74 75 76 77 78 79

70 + 3 = _____   79 + 0 = _____   77 + 1 = _____

78 + 0 = _____   70 + 2 = _____   74 + 2 = _____

76 + 1 = _____   78 + 1 = _____   76 + 2 = _____

72 + 2 = _____   71 + 3 = _____   75 + 1 = _____

© MM, Alpha Omega Publications, Inc.

3 Look at the flowers. Color one space on the graph for each flower.

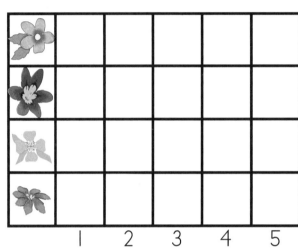

| | 1 | 2 | 3 | 4 | 5 |

4 Write the numbers.

place value
tens | ones

33 = tens [ ] ones [ ]   36 = tens [ ] ones [ ]

34 = _____ tens and _____ ones.

38 = _____ tens and _____ ones.

30 = _____ tens and _____ ones.

Horizons Math K Book 2

Lesson 98

front   back

50 cents   50¢

A half dollar is worth 50¢. Two half dollars are equal to $1.

1 Find the value of each set of coins.

= _____ ¢

= _____ ¢

= _____ ¢

2 Write the number after.

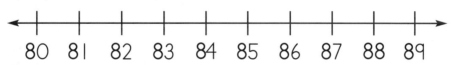

80 81 82 83 84 85 86 87 88 89

83 _____	87 _____	88 _____
86 _____	82 _____	84 _____
80 _____	85 _____	81 _____

3 Add.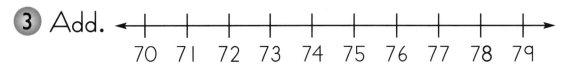

70 71 72 73 74 75 76 77 78 79

```
  74        72        70        75
+  3      +  1      +  0      +  3
```

```
  77        71        78        70
+  2      +  4      +  1      +  2
```

```
  75        76        73        71
+  0      +  3      +  2      +  2
```

4 Match the place each car is in.

4th

1st

2nd

5th

3rd

6th

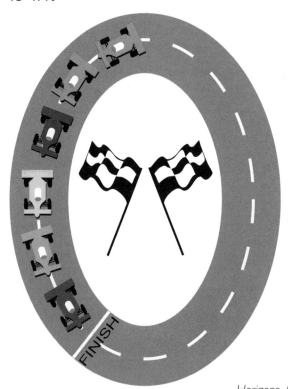

Horizons Math K Book 2

Lesson 99

1 Match the season with the correct picture.

Summer

Fall

Winter

Spring

2 Circle the correct number of coins.

     = 50 ¢

        = 50 ¢

3 Write the number after.

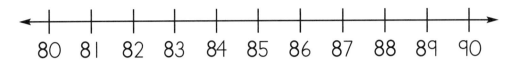

80 81 82 83 84 85 86 87 88 89 90

89 _____	81 _____	88 _____
80 _____	85 _____	82 _____
86 _____	83 _____	84 _____

4 Add.

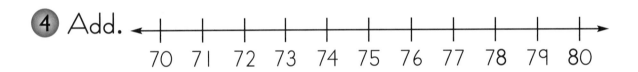

70 71 72 73 74 75 76 77 78 79 80

71 + 6 = _____   73 + 2 = _____   76 + 2 = _____

75 + 3 = _____   70 + 4 = _____   78 + 2 = _____

71 + 6 = _____   77 + 2 = _____   75 + 2 = _____

70 + 3 = _____   72 + 7 = _____   74 + 5 = _____

© MM, Alpha Omega Publications, Inc.

Lesson 100

1 Add.

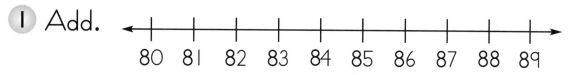

80 81 82 83 84 85 86 87 88 89

84	88	81	83	82
+ 1	+ 1	+ 3	+ 2	+ 1

85	86	87	80	84
+ 3	+ 1	+ 1	+ 3	+ 2

2 Count to 100.

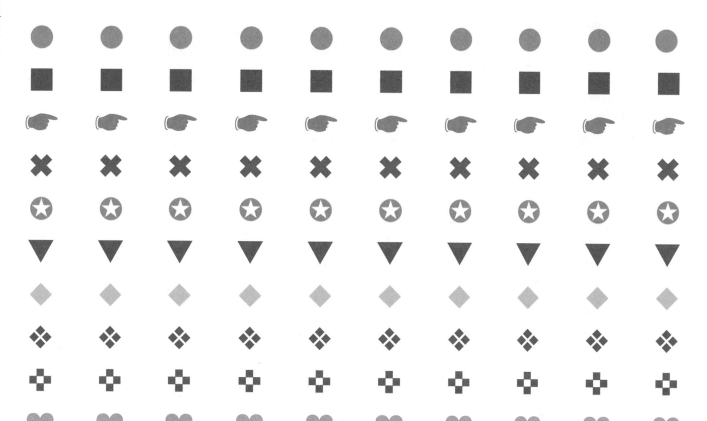

3 Count the coins.

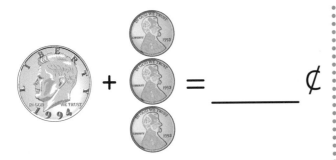

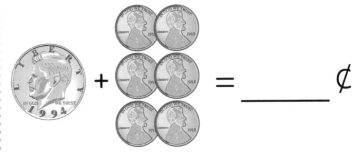

4 Write the time in the blanks.

4:00

The time is _____ o'clock.
One hour before is _____ o'clock.
One hour after is _____ o'clock.

The time is _____ o'clock.
One hour before is _____ o'clock.
One hour after is _____ o'clock.

The time is _____ o'clock.
One hour before is _____ o'clock.
One hour after is _____ o'clock.

The time is _____ o'clock.
One hour before is _____ o'clock.
One hour after is _____ o'clock.

Horizons Math K Book 2

Lesson 101

1 Bob has 2 toy cars. Jim has 3 toy cars. How many cars do they have altogether?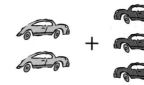

Bob + Jim = _____ + _____ = _____

Mom has 1 jar. Dad has 2 jars. How many jars do they have altogether?

Mom + Dad = _____ + _____ = _____ jars

June has 30 days. May has 1 more. How many days are in May?

June + 1 = _____ + _____ = _____ days

2 Add.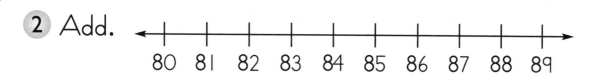

$85 + 2 =$ _____ $80 + 3 =$ _____ $85 + 0 =$ _____

$84 + 1 =$ _____ $81 + 3 =$ _____ $84 + 2 =$ _____

$87 + 2 =$ _____ $82 + 3 =$ _____ $87 + 1 =$ _____

$86 + 1 =$ _____ $83 + 3 =$ _____ $86 + 2 =$ _____

3 Write the numbers on the clock.

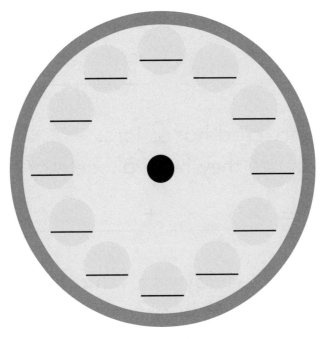

4 Add.

2 + 1	3 + 2	4 + 0	5 + 1
9 + 0	8 + 1	7 + 1	6 + 2
1 + 1	2 + 2	3 + 3	4 + 4

Lesson 102

_____

1 How many hours?

 _____ hours

 _____ hours

 _____ hours

 _____ hours

2 Bill rides his bike for 5 minutes. Jim rides his bike  for 3 minutes. How many minutes do they ride altogether?

_____ + _____ = _____ minutes

Sal has 2 dolls. Deb has 4 dolls.
How many dolls do they have altogether?

_____ + _____ = _____ dolls

Dot is a dog with 1 spot. Bo is a cat with 3 spots.
How many spots do they have altogether?

_____ + _____ = _____ spots

3 Count by 2's.

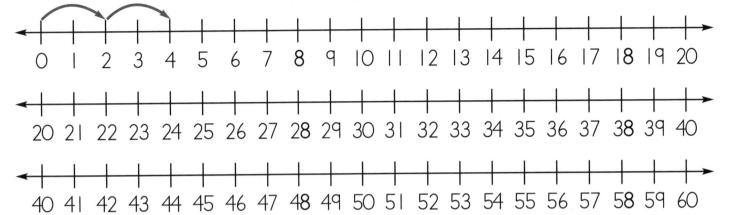

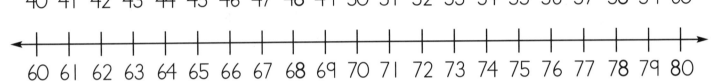

4 Add.

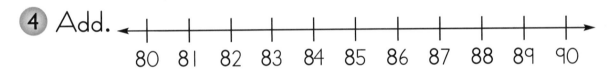

80 + 3	85 + 2	83 + 1	86 + 2
89 + 1	81 + 3	82 + 5	81 + 6
83 + 5	82 + 7	80 + 4	84 + 5

Horizons Math K Book 2

Lesson 103

① Write the number.

front　　back　　front　　back

1 dollar　　$1.00

100 = $1.00

20 = $1.00

10 = $1.00

2 = $1.00

_____ =

_____ =

_____ =

_____ =

② Write the number of hours.

 _____ hours

 _____ hours

 _____ hours

 _____ hours

Horizons Math K Book 2

3 Write the number.

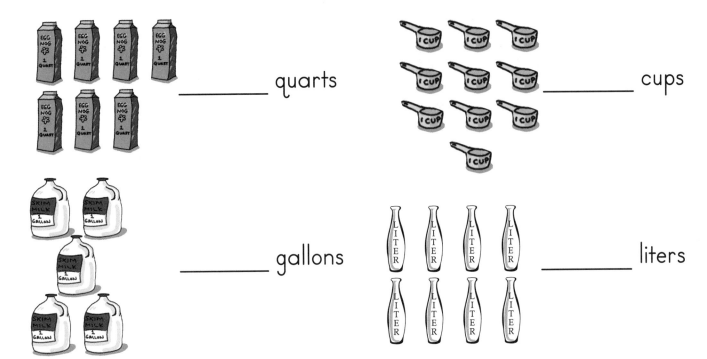

_____ quarts

_____ cups

_____ gallons

_____ liters

4 Count by 2's.

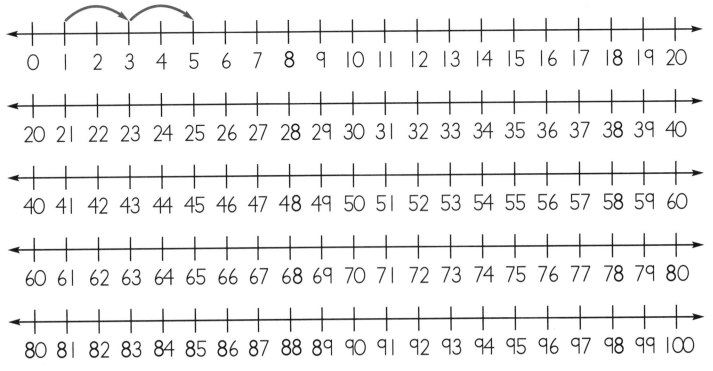

© MM, Alpha Omega Publications, Inc.

Lesson 104

1 Color one half of each shape.

 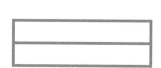 

2 Write the amount.

 = $ _____

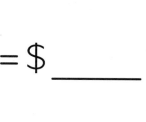 = $ _____

 = $ _____

 = $ _____

3 Circle the odd numbers.

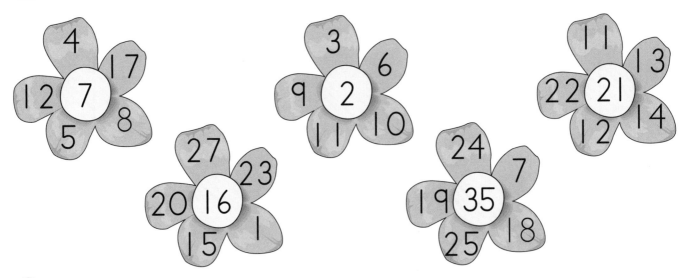

4 Write the number.

4 quarts = 1 gallon

_____ quarts = _____ gallons

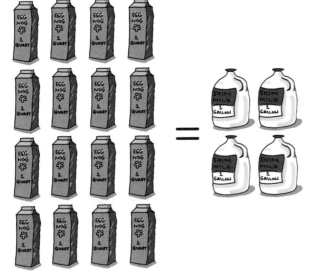

_____ quarts = _____ gallons

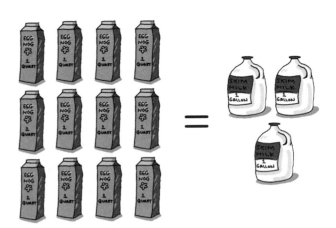

_____ quarts = _____ gallons

Lesson 105

1 Circle the clocks that show half past the hour.

8 o'clock

half past 8 o'clock

2 How many equal parts?

_____   _____   _____   _____

      +

_____   _____   _____   _____

3 Write the amount.

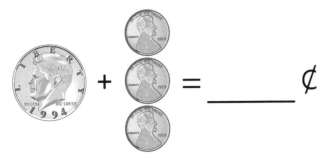 +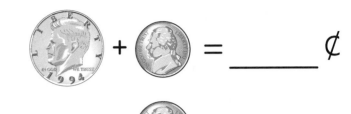

= _____ ¢   = _____ ¢

 +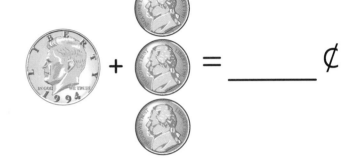

= _____ ¢   = _____ ¢

4 Find the perimeter.

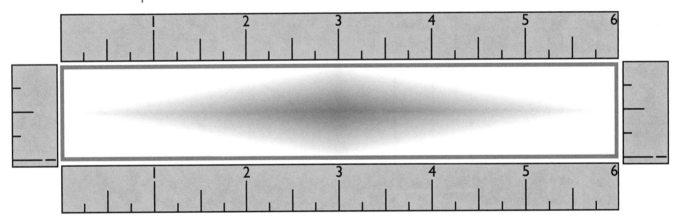

_____ inches

5 Circle the 4th month. Put an X on the 7th month. Draw a rectangle around the 10th month.

January	February	March	April
May	June	July	August
September	October	November	December

© MM, Alpha Omega Publications, Inc.

Horizons Math K Book 2

50

Lesson 106

1 When we take something away, the answer is less.

3 – 1 = _____   2 – 1 = _____   4 – 2 = _____

3 – 2 = _____   2 – 2 = _____   4 – 1 = _____

2 Write the time.

half past _____   half past _____   half past _____

half past _____   half past _____   half past _____

3 Draw a line to make each whole into 2 halves.

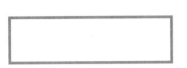  

4 Write the amount.

 = _____ ¢   = _____ ¢

 = $ _____    = $ _____

 = _____ ¢    = _____ ¢

Lesson 107

1 Write the number between.

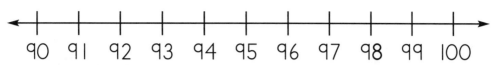

| 90 | 91 | 92 | 93 | 94 | 95 | 96 | 97 | 98 | 99 | 100 |

93 _____ 95   97 _____ 99   91 _____ 93

94 _____ 96   98 _____ 100   90 _____ 92

95 _____ 97   92 _____ 94   96 _____ 98

2 When we take away nothing, the answer is the same.

3 − 0 = _____   2 − 0 = _____   4 − 0 = _____

9 − 0 = _____   7 − 0 = _____   5 − 0 = _____

③ Draw lines to the correct time.

2:30

5:30

9:30

© MM, Alpha Omega Publications, Inc.

④ Circle the number of halves needed to make a whole.

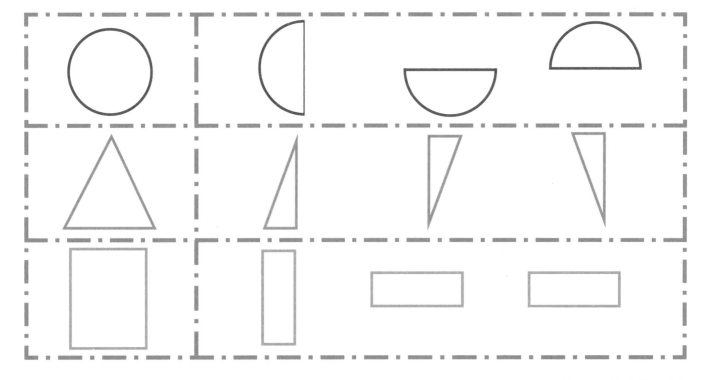

Lesson 108

1 Write the number after.

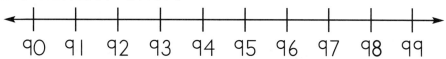

| 90 | 91 | 92 | 93 | 94 | 95 | 96 | 97 | 98 | 99 |

| 97 _____ | 95 _____ | 90 _____ |

| 94 _____ | 98 _____ | 91 _____ |

| 96 _____ | 92 _____ | 93 _____ |

2 Write the number between.

| 90 _____ 92 | 96 _____ 98 | 95 _____ 97 |

| 92 _____ 94 | 91 _____ 93 | 94 _____ 96 |

3 When you take away, the answer is the same or less.

4 – 2 = _____   8 – 3 = _____   2 – 1 = _____

9 – 0 = _____   7 – 3 = _____   3 – 3 = _____

④ Add.

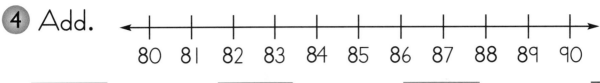

80 81 82 83 84 85 86 87 88 89 90

```
  81        86        82        80
+  4      +  3      +  7      +  6
```

place value

tens | ones

⑤ Write the numbers.

31 = _____ tens and _____ ones

39 = _____ tens and _____ ones

35 = _____ tens and _____ ones

⑥ Match the person by the place in line.

5th   8th   2nd   4th   1st   7th   3rd   6th

Lesson 109

1 Subtract.

6 − 2 = _____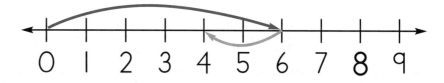

8 − 3 = _____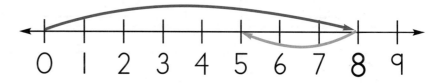

14 − 2 = _____

17 − 1 = _____

2 Circle every 3rd number.

	1	2	3	4	5	6	7	8	9
10	11	12	13	14	15	16	17	18	19
20	21	22	23	24	25	26	27	28	29
30	31	32	33	34	35	36	37	38	39
40	41	42	43	44	45	46	47	48	49

3 Write the number after.

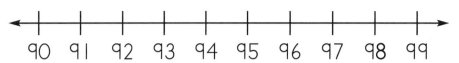

90 91 92 93 94 95 96 97 98 99

| 94 ____ | 90 ____ | 96 ____ |
| 93 ____ | 97 ____ | 91 ____ |

4 Write the number between.

| 97 ____ 99 | 91 ____ 93 | 95 ____ 97 |
| 90 ____ 92 | 96 ____ 98 | 93 ____ 95 |

5 Look at the chart to see the time that the children get home.

Tom	Bess	JoAnn
9:00	2:00	4:00

a. When does Bess get home? _____:_____

b. When does Tom get home? _____:_____

c. When does JoAnn get home? _____:_____

Lesson 110

1 Write the number before.

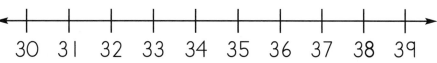

30 31 32 33 34 35 36 37 38 39

_____ 32	_____ 35	_____ 39
_____ 31	_____ 34	_____ 38
_____ 36	_____ 33	_____ 37

2 Count by 3's.

| | 6 | | 12 | 18 | | 24 | | 30 | 36 |

3 Subtract.

17 – 3 = _____

10 11 12 13 14 15 16 17 18 19

14 – 0 = _____

10 11 12 13 14 15 16 17 18 19

19 – 2 = _____

10 11 12 13 14 15 16 17 18 19

13 – 3 = _____

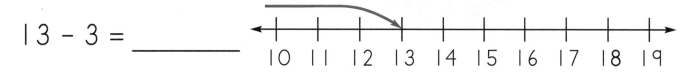

10 11 12 13 14 15 16 17 18 19

© MM, Alpha Omega Publications, Inc.

④ Circle the correct order for the days of the week.

Saturday   Monday   Wednesday   Friday   Sunday   Tuesday   Thursday

Sunday   Monday   Tuesday   Wednesday   Thursday   Friday   Saturday

Saturday   Friday   Thursday   Wednesday   Tuesday   Monday   Sunday

⑤ Add.

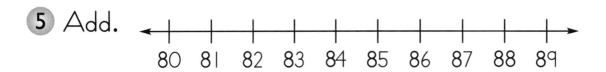

80   81   82   83   84   85   86   87   88   89

81 + 6 = ____   86 + 3 = ____

85 + 4 = ____   87 + 2 = ____

80 + 7 = ____   81 + 5 = ____

82 + 6 = ____   84 + 4 = ____

Lesson 111

1 Add.

90 91 92 93 94 95 96 97 98 99

90 + 1 = _____   97 + 0 = _____   94 + 2 = _____

96 + 2 = _____   95 + 1 = _____   91 + 2 = _____

93 + 1 = _____   98 + 0 = _____   90 + 2 = _____

2 Count by 3's.

3		9		15		
24		30		36		42
	48			57		
66		72		78		
	90		96			

3 Subtract.

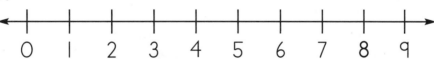

0 1 2 3 4 5 6 7 8 9

$$\begin{array}{r} 4 \\ -\ 1 \\ \hline \end{array} \quad \begin{array}{r} 2 \\ -\ 0 \\ \hline \end{array} \quad \begin{array}{r} 3 \\ -\ 1 \\ \hline \end{array} \quad \begin{array}{r} 6 \\ -\ 0 \\ \hline \end{array} \quad \begin{array}{r} 7 \\ -\ 1 \\ \hline \end{array} \quad \begin{array}{r} 1 \\ -\ 1 \\ \hline \end{array}$$

4 Add.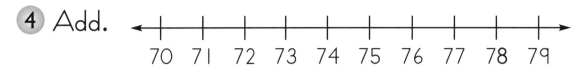

70 71 72 73 74 75 76 77 78 79

$$72 + 6$$ $$77 + 2$$ $$71 + 5$$ $$75 + 4$$ $$70 + 7$$

$$73 + 4$$ $$76 + 2$$ $$72 + 5$$ $$70 + 4$$ $$78 + 1$$

5 Subtract.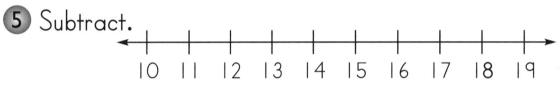

10 11 12 13 14 15 16 17 18 19

$12 - 2 =$ _____ $13 - 1 =$ _____ $19 - 2 =$ _____

$17 - 1 =$ _____ $11 - 0 =$ _____ $14 - 1 =$ _____

$18 - 2 =$ _____ $15 - 2 =$ _____ $10 - 0 =$ _____

6 Write the number before.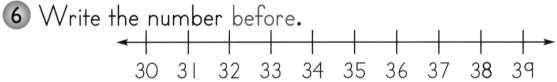

30 31 32 33 34 35 36 37 38 39

_____ 33	_____ 36	_____ 39
_____ 31	_____ 34	_____ 37
_____ 32	_____ 38	_____ 36

Lesson 112

1 Color one third of each shape.

Color one fourth of each shape.

   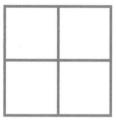

2 Add.

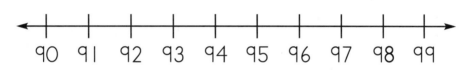

```
 92        97        94        91
+  3      +  2      +  3      +  4
____      ____      ____      ____
```

```
 90        96        98        95
+  3      +  2      +  1      +  3
____      ____      ____      ____
```

```
 92        93        96        91
+  2      +  0      +  3      +  2
____      ____      ____      ____
```

3 Dad has 3 pens. Kim has 2 pens. How many pens do they have altogether? 3 + 2 = _____ pens.

8 ducks are in the lake. A big duck lands in the lake. Now there are _____ ducks in the lake altogether. Ben does not have a cat. His dad brings a cat home from the pound. Then Ben has _____ cat in all.

4 Write the number before.

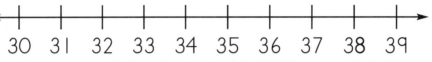

30   31   32   33   34   35   36   37   38   39

_____ 32	_____ 31	_____ 33
_____ 36	_____ 39	_____ 38
_____ 34	_____ 35	_____ 37

5 Subtract.

10   11   12   13   14   15   16   17   18   19

| 19 | 16 | 15 | 11 |
| − 3 | − 2 | − 3 | − 1 |

| 14 | 17 | 18 | 12 |
| − 3 | − 2 | − 1 | − 0 |

Lesson 113

1 Subtract.

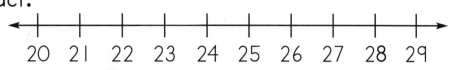

20 21 22 23 24 25 26 27 28 29

```
  24        28        27        22
-  1      -  1      -  0      -  2
```

```
  23        25        29        26
-  1      -  0      -  2      -  1
```

2 Write the number of equal parts under each shape.

_____   _____   _____

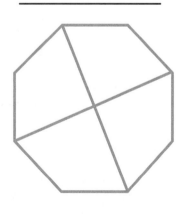   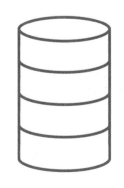   

_____   _____   _____

Horizons Math K Book 2

65

3 Add.

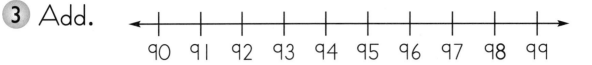

90 91 92 93 94 95 96 97 98 99

92 + 4 = _____   97 + 1 = _____   90 + 3 = _____

95 + 2 = _____   93 + 6 = _____   91 + 4 = _____

94 + 4 = _____   98 + 1 = _____   96 + 3 = _____

4 Count by 2's.

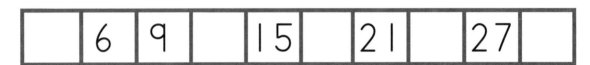

| | 4 | | | 10 | | 14 | | | 20 |

Count by 3's.

| | 6 | 9 | | 15 | | 21 | | 27 | |

5 Subtract.

10 11 12 13 14 15 16 17 18 19

16 – 2 = _____   13 – 1 = _____   15 – 2 = _____

11 – 1 = _____   14 – 2 = _____   18 – 3 = _____

17 – 2 = _____   10 – 0 = _____   12 – 1 = _____

Horizons Math K Book 2

Lesson 114

A quarter dollar is worth 25¢.
4 quarter dollars are equal to $1.

front   back
25 cents   25¢

1 Find the value of each set of coins.

 = $ _____    = _____ ¢

 = _____ ¢    = _____ ¢

2 Subtract.

```
 +---+---+---+---+---+---+---+---+---+---+
 20  21  22  23  24  25  26  27  28  29
```

26 − 2 = _____   23 − 1 = _____   29 − 3 = _____

25 − 1 = _____   24 − 2 = _____   21 − 1 = _____

26 − 0 = _____   22 − 1 = _____   28 − 3 = _____

3 Circle the ones that show equal parts.

 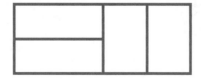

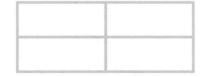 

4 Add.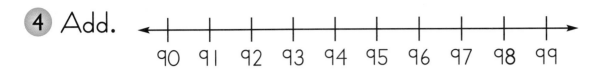

90   91   92   93   94   95   96   97   98   99

```
   90        94        92        97
+   6     +   5     +   4     +   2
```

```
   95        93        91        96
+   3     +   5     +   4     +   2
```

5 Subtract.

0   1   2   3   4   5   6   7   8   9

```
    6         4         3         7
-   1     -   0     -   1     -   2
```

```
    9         6         8         2
-   1     -   2     -   0     -   1
```

Lesson 115

1 Write the numbers.

44 = _____ tens and _____ ones.

41 = _____ tens and _____ ones.

_____ = 4 tens and 6 ones.

_____ = 4 tens and 0 ones.

2 Find the value.

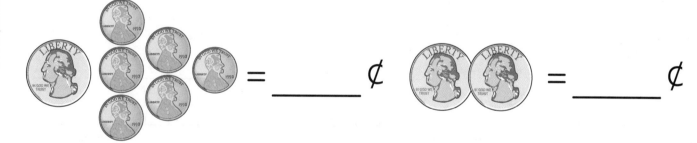

= _____ ¢   = _____ ¢

= $ _____

= _____ ¢

3 Match the season.

Summer

Fall

Winter

Spring

4 Color one equal part in each shape.

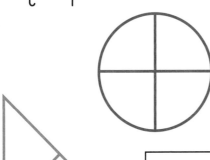
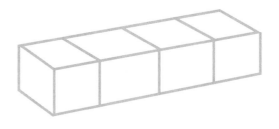

5 Subtract.

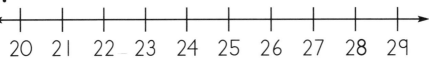

25 – 5 = _____   28 – 3 = _____   22 – 1 = _____

27 – 4 = _____   24 – 2 = _____   29 – 6 = _____

21 – 0 = _____   25 – 4 = _____   28 – 5 = _____

Horizons Math K Book 2

© MM, Alpha Omega Publications, Inc.

Lesson 116

1 Subtract.

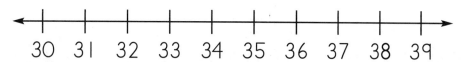

30 31 32 33 34 35 36 37 38 39

32 – 1 = _____   37 – 2 = _____   34 – 1 = _____

35 – 0 = _____   32 – 2 = _____   38 – 1 = _____

39 – 2 = _____   33 – 2 = _____   36 – 1 = _____

2 Write the numbers.

place value
tens | ones

46 = _____ tens and _____ ones.

_____ = 4 tens and 9 ones.

44 = _____ tens and _____ ones.

_____ = 4 tens and 1 one.

3 Find the value.

 = _____ ¢

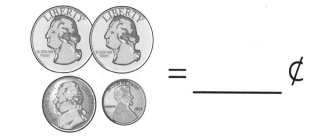 = _____ ¢

4 Find the perimeter.

_____ inches

5 Subtract.

```
   21          24          28          30
 -  1        -  3        -  4        -  2
```

```
   23          20          25          27
 -  2        -  1        -  3        -  4
```

Lesson 117

1 Write the number before.

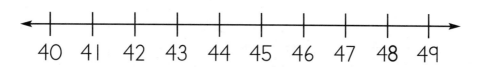

40 41 42 43 44 45 46 47 48 49

_____ 44	_____ 48	_____ 41
_____ 47	_____ 44	_____ 42
_____ 46	_____ 43	_____ 45

2 Subtract.

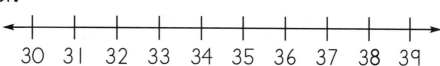

30 31 32 33 34 35 36 37 38 39

```
  36        34        38        37
-  2      -  3      -  2      -  0
____      ____      ____      ____
```

```
  31        37        33        39
-  0      -  3      -  2      -  2
____      ____      ____      ____
```

© MM, Alpha Omega Publications, Inc.

3 Count by 2's.

| 20 | | 24 | | 28 | 30 | | 34 | | 38 |

Count by 3's.

| 3 | 6 | | 12 | 15 | | 21 | 24 | | 30 |

Count by 10's.

| 10 | | | 40 | | 60 | | | | 100 |

4 Circle coins in each row to equal the first coin.

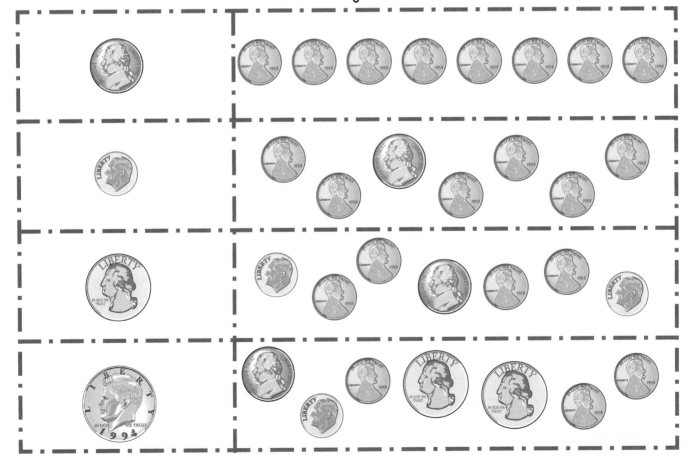

Lesson 118

1 Circle the spheres and cones.

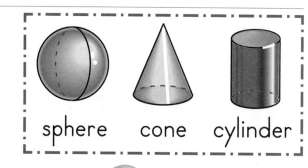

sphere   cone   cylinder

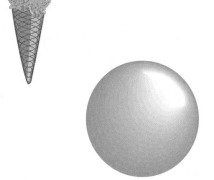

2 Write the number before.

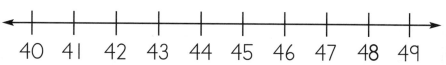

40 41 42 43 44 45 46 47 48 49

_____ 48	_____ 42	_____ 44
_____ 45	_____ 41	_____ 49
_____ 46	_____ 43	_____ 47

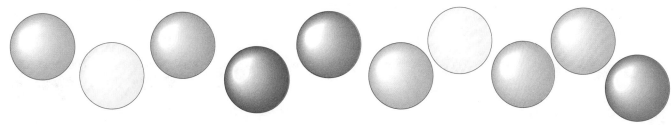

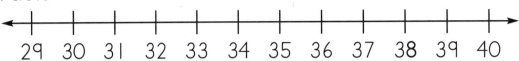

3 Subtract.

35 – 3 = _____   32 – 3 = _____   40 – 5 = _____

37 – 2 = _____   34 – 4 = _____   33 – 3 = _____

36 – 6 = _____   35 – 5 = _____   38 – 6 = _____

4 Write the number.

 _____ quarts

 _____ liters

 _____ cups

 _____ gallons

 = _____

© MM, Alpha Omega Publications, Inc.

Horizons Math K Book 2

Lesson 119

There are 4 quarters in a dollar. Do you know about quarter-hours, too? This clock face shows a quarter of an hour. It is also called 15 minutes.

1 Write the numbers on this clock face. Draw the minute hand and the hour hand to show 8:15.

2 Circle the spheres.

Circle the cylinders.

© MM, Alpha Omega Publications, Inc.

3 Write the number before.

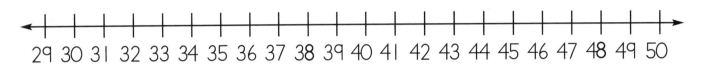

29 30 31 32 33 34 35 36 37 38 39 40 41 42 43 44 45 46 47 48 49 50

| _____ 44 | _____ 37 | _____ 48 |

| _____ 32 | _____ 41 | _____ 34 |

| _____ 46 | _____ 30 | _____ 50 |

4 Subtract.

```
  33        39        35        37
-  3      -  4      -  3      -  5
____      ____      ____      ____
```

```
  36        34        38        40
-  0      -  5      -  4      -  5
____      ____      ____      ____
```

Lesson 120

1 Write the numbers.

52 = _____ tens and _____ ones.

_____ = 5 tens and 8 ones.

56 = _____ tens and _____ ones.

_____ = 5 tens and 4 ones.

2 Circle spheres, cones and cylinders.
Some have more than one.

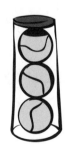

3 Color the graph for the number of each coin.

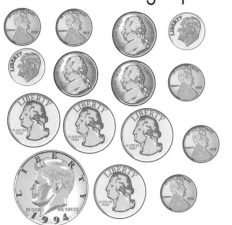
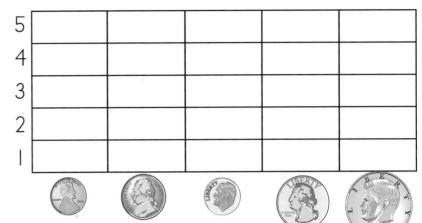

4 From the 12 to the 3 is 15 minutes.

Make the hands show 5:15.

____ minutes after ____ o'clock

____ minutes after ____ o'clock

5 Subtract.

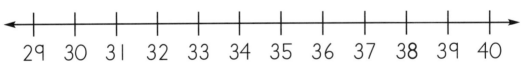

36 – 3 = _____   40 – 3 = _____   33 – 3 = _____

36 – 2 = _____   40 – 2 = _____   33 – 2 = _____

36 – 4 = _____   40 – 4 = _____   33 – 4 = _____

Horizons Math K Book 2

Lesson 121

① Subtract.

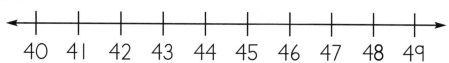

40 41 42 43 44 45 46 47 48 49

```
  42
-  1
____
```

```
  48
-  2
____
```

```
  46
-  0
____
```

```
  49
-  1
____
```

```
  45
-  2
____
```

```
  43
-  1
____
```

```
  44
-  0
____
```

```
  47
-  2
____
```

```
  41
-  1
____
```

```
  48
-  0
____
```

```
  43
-  2
____
```

```
  46
-  2
____
```

place value

tens | ones

② Write the numbers.

59 = _____ tens and _____ ones.

50 = _____ tens and _____ ones.

_____ = 5 tens and 3 ones.

_____ = 5 tens and 7 ones.

3 Make the hands and write the time.

2:15

9:15

10:15

____ minutes after

____ o'clock

____ minutes after

____ o'clock

____ minutes after

____ o'clock

4 Add.

$$1 + 0$$

$$1 + 1$$

$$2 + 0$$

$$2 + 1$$

$$2 + 2$$

$$3 + 0$$

$$3 + 1$$

$$3 + 2$$

$$3 + 3$$

$$4 + 0$$

$$4 + 1$$

$$4 + 2$$

$$4 + 3$$

$$4 + 4$$

$$5 + 0$$

$$5 + 1$$

$$5 + 2$$

$$5 + 3$$

$$5 + 4$$

Lesson 122

1 Write the number **before**.

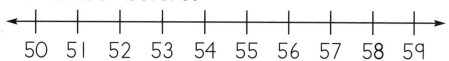

50	51	52	53	54	55	56	57	58	59

_____ 51   _____ 59   _____ 52

_____ 58   _____ 53   _____ 57

_____ 54   _____ 56   _____ 55

2 Subtract.

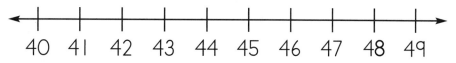

40	41	42	43	44	45	46	47	48	49

41 – 0 = _____   45 – 1 = _____   42 – 1 = _____

46 – 2 = _____   43 – 0 = _____   47 – 1 = _____

44 – 1 = _____   48 – 2 = _____   45 – 0 = _____

47 – 0 = _____   41 – 1 = _____   44 – 2 = _____

© MM, Alpha Omega Publications, Inc.

3 Circle the coins needed to buy each item.

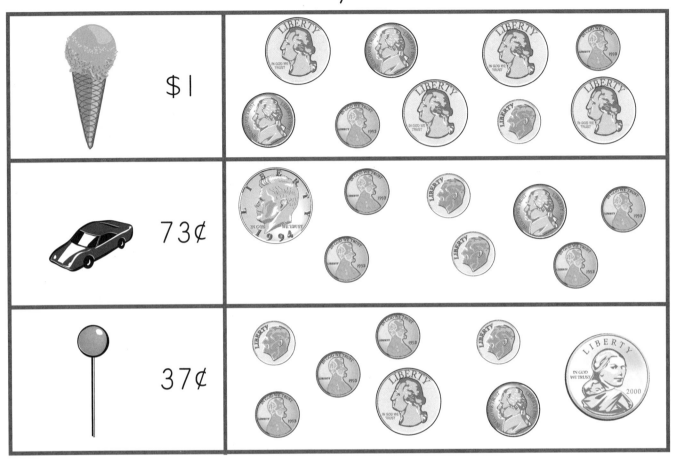

4 Your digital clock has quarter-hours, too!
It shows 15 minutes. Write the time.

2:00

___:___

15 minutes later

5:00

___:___

15 minutes later

Lesson 123

place value
tens | ones

1 Write the numbers.

66 = _____ tens and _____ ones.

63 = _____ tens and _____ ones.

_____ = 6 tens and 8 ones.

_____ = 6 tens and 1 one.

2 Write the number before.

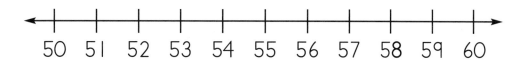

50 51 52 53 54 55 56 57 58 59 60

____60	____55	____51
____59	____56	____52
____58	____54	____57

3 Subtract.

```
   44        48        42        49
 -  3      -  5      -  2      -  6
```

```
   47        45        50        41
 -  4      -  3      -  5      -  1
```

4 Write the time.

11:00   **8:00**   **3:00**

15 minutes later   15 minutes later   one-quarter hour later

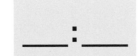

__ __ : __ __   __ __ : __ __   __ __ : __ __

Horizons Math K Book 2

Lesson 124

1 Count by 4's and trace the numbers.

1	2	3	4	5	6	7	8	9	10
11	12	13	14	15	16	17	18	19	20
21	22	23	24	25	26	27	28	29	30
31	32	33	34	35	36	37	38	39	40
41	42	43	44	45	46	47	48	49	50
51	52	53	54	55	56	57	58	59	60
61	62	63	64	65	66	67	68	69	70
71	72	73	74	75	76	77	78	79	80
81	82	83	84	85	86	87	88	89	90
91	92	93	94	95	96	97	98	99	100

2 Write the numbers.

place value

tens | ones

_____ = 6 tens and 2 ones.

_____ = 6 tens and 6 ones.

69 = _____ tens and _____ ones.

61 = _____ tens and _____ ones.

3 Write the number before.

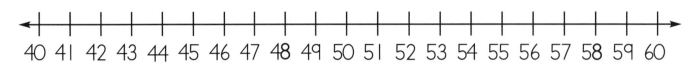

40 41 42 43 44 45 46 47 48 49 50 51 52 53 54 55 56 57 58 59 60

_____ 55

_____ 45

_____ 52

_____ 42

_____ 57

_____ 47

_____ 53

_____ 49

_____ 60

4 Subtract.

40   41   42   43   44   45   46   47   48   49   50

50 – 6 = _____

45 – 4 = _____

48 – 3 = _____

43 – 3 = _____

46 – 0 = _____

49 – 8 = _____

50 – 5 = _____

47 – 6 = _____

42 – 2 = _____

Horizons Math K Book 2

Lesson 125

1 Subtract.

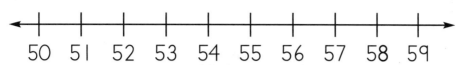

50 51 52 53 54 55 56 57 58 59

50 – 0 = _____   51 – 1 = _____   52 – 1 = _____

54 – 1 = _____   53 – 2 = _____   56 – 2 = _____

52 – 2 = _____   58 – 0 = _____   53 – 1 = _____

55 – 1 = _____   57 – 2 = _____   58 – 2 = _____

2 Count by 4's.

4	8	12	16	20	24	28	32

36	40	44	48	52	56	60	64

68	72	76	80	84	88	92	96

Horizons Math K Book 2

place value
tens | ones

3 Write the numbers.

33 = _____ tens and _____ ones.

46 = _____ tens and _____ ones.

67 = _____ tens and _____ ones.

52 = _____ tens and _____ ones.

4 Circle the correct digital time.

Horizons Math K Book 2

Lesson 126

1 Write the number before.

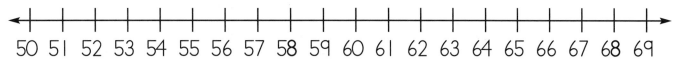

50 51 52 53 54 55 56 57 58 59 60 61 62 63 64 65 66 67 68 69

_____ 66	_____ 63	_____ 68
_____ 64	_____ 61	_____ 67
_____ 62	_____ 65	_____ 69

2 Subtract.

$$\begin{array}{r} 56 \\ -\ 2 \\ \hline \end{array}$$ $$\begin{array}{r} 58 \\ -\ 2 \\ \hline \end{array}$$ $$\begin{array}{r} 54 \\ -\ 2 \\ \hline \end{array}$$ $$\begin{array}{r} 59 \\ -\ 2 \\ \hline \end{array}$$

$$\begin{array}{r} 57 \\ -\ 3 \\ \hline \end{array}$$ $$\begin{array}{r} 59 \\ -\ 3 \\ \hline \end{array}$$ $$\begin{array}{r} 55 \\ -\ 3 \\ \hline \end{array}$$ $$\begin{array}{r} 60 \\ -\ 3 \\ \hline \end{array}$$

$$\begin{array}{r} 58 \\ -\ 4 \\ \hline \end{array}$$ $$\begin{array}{r} 60 \\ -\ 4 \\ \hline \end{array}$$ $$\begin{array}{r} 56 \\ -\ 4 \\ \hline \end{array}$$ $$\begin{array}{r} 57 \\ -\ 4 \\ \hline \end{array}$$

③ Count by 4's and circle the numbers.

1	2	3	4	5	6	7	8	9	10
11	12	13	14	15	16	17	18	19	20
21	22	23	24	25	26	27	28	29	30
31	32	33	34	35	36	37	38	39	40
41	42	43	44	45	46	47	48	49	50
51	52	53	54	55	56	57	58	59	60
61	62	63	64	65	66	67	68	69	70
71	72	73	74	75	76	77	78	79	80
81	82	83	84	85	86	87	88	89	90
91	92	93	94	95	96	97	98	99	100

④ Add or subtract.

$$\begin{array}{r} 2 \\ -\ 1 \\ \hline \end{array} \qquad \begin{array}{r} 3 \\ -\ 0 \\ \hline \end{array} \qquad \begin{array}{r} 4 \\ -\ 1 \\ \hline \end{array} \qquad \begin{array}{r} 7 \\ -\ 2 \\ \hline \end{array} \qquad \begin{array}{r} 4 \\ -\ 1 \\ \hline \end{array}$$

$$\begin{array}{r} 1 \\ +\ 2 \\ \hline \end{array} \qquad \begin{array}{r} 1 \\ +\ 3 \\ \hline \end{array} \qquad \begin{array}{r} 2 \\ +\ 1 \\ \hline \end{array} \qquad \begin{array}{r} 3 \\ +\ 1 \\ \hline \end{array} \qquad \begin{array}{r} 2 \\ +\ 2 \\ \hline \end{array}$$

Horizons Math K Book 2

Lesson 127

1 Subtract.

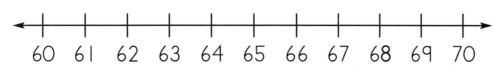

60   61   62   63   64   65   66   67   68   69   70

| 69 | 64 | 67 | 63 |
| - 1 | - 2 | - 1 | - 1 |

| 68 | 66 | 62 | 61 |
| - 0 | - 2 | - 1 | - 1 |

| 65 | 67 | 63 | 68 |
| - 2 | - 2 | - 3 | - 2 |

2 Sue has 3 lollipops. She eats 1 lollipop.

She will have _____ lollipops left.

Mom has 6 eggs. She puts 3 eggs in a cake mix.

Mom has _____ eggs left.

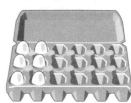

3 Fill in the numbers to complete each row.

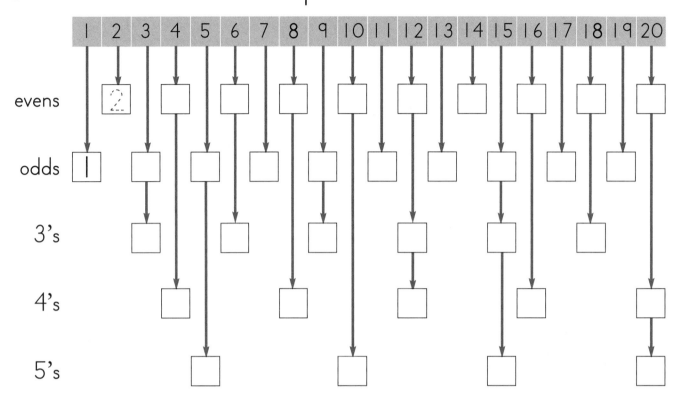

	1	2	3	4	5	6	7	8	9	10	11	12	13	14	15	16	17	18	19	20
evens		2																		
odds	1																			
3's																				
4's																				
5's																				

4 Complete these rows from the chart above.

2	4	6							

1	3	5							

3	6				

4	8			

5			

Horizons Math K Book 2

Lesson 128

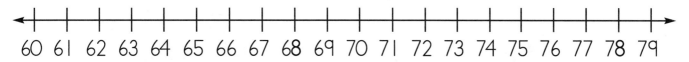

1 Write the number before.

$$\longleftarrow \overset{\quad|\quad|\quad|\quad|\quad|\quad|\quad|\quad|\quad|\quad|\quad|\quad|\quad|\quad|\quad|\quad|\quad|\quad|\quad|\quad|}{} \longrightarrow$$
60 61 62 63 64 65 66 67 68 69 70 71 72 73 74 75 76 77 78 79

| _____ 71 | _____ 76 | _____ 79 |

| _____ 78 | _____ 72 | _____ 75 |

| _____ 73 | _____ 74 | _____ 77 |

2 Subtract.

$68 - 1 = \underline{\hspace{1cm}}$ $63 - 2 = \underline{\hspace{1cm}}$ $67 - 3 = \underline{\hspace{1cm}}$

$65 - 3 = \underline{\hspace{1cm}}$ $61 - 0 = \underline{\hspace{1cm}}$ $62 - 1 = \underline{\hspace{1cm}}$

$66 - 0 = \underline{\hspace{1cm}}$ $68 - 4 = \underline{\hspace{1cm}}$ $63 - 3 = \underline{\hspace{1cm}}$

$67 - 3 = \underline{\hspace{1cm}}$ $64 - 2 = \underline{\hspace{1cm}}$ $69 - 5 = \underline{\hspace{1cm}}$

3 Match the clocks.

3:30

7:15

2:15

9:30

4 Choose the correct word from the word bank.

Fall begins in _____ .

Spring begins in _____ .

Winter starts in _____ .

Summer starts in _____ .

WORD BANK					
January	February	March	April	May	June
July	August	September	October	November	December

Lesson 129

1 Subtract.

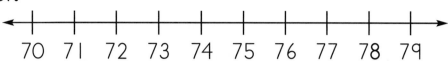

$$74 - 1 = \underline{\hspace{2cm}} \qquad 72 - 0 = \underline{\hspace{2cm}} \qquad 77 - 2 = \underline{\hspace{2cm}}$$

$$73 - 2 = \underline{\hspace{2cm}} \qquad 71 - 1 = \underline{\hspace{2cm}} \qquad 79 - 3 = \underline{\hspace{2cm}}$$

$$75 - 1 = \underline{\hspace{2cm}} \qquad 78 - 2 = \underline{\hspace{2cm}} \qquad 76 - 1 = \underline{\hspace{2cm}}$$

2 Match the shapes.

3 Subtract.

```
  20          16          17          19
-  4        -  4        -  3        -  3
```

```
  15          18          17          20
-  5        -  5        -  6        -  6
```

4 Write the missing numbers.

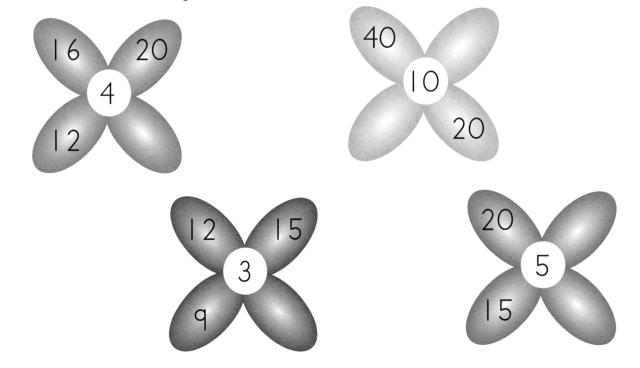

Lesson 130

1 Write the number before.

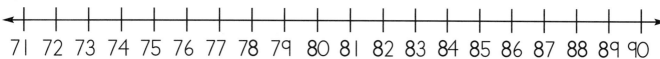

| 71 | 72 | 73 | 74 | 75 | 76 | 77 | 78 | 79 | 80 | 81 | 82 | 83 | 84 | 85 | 86 | 87 | 88 | 89 | 90 |

_____ 84	_____ 89	_____ 83
_____ 87	_____ 85	_____ 88
_____ 81	_____ 90	_____ 86

2 Subtract.

$$\begin{array}{r} 78 \\ -3 \\ \hline \end{array} \qquad \begin{array}{r} 74 \\ -2 \\ \hline \end{array} \qquad \begin{array}{r} 78 \\ -4 \\ \hline \end{array} \qquad \begin{array}{r} 73 \\ -3 \\ \hline \end{array}$$

$$\begin{array}{r} 79 \\ -5 \\ \hline \end{array} \qquad \begin{array}{r} 75 \\ -3 \\ \hline \end{array} \qquad \begin{array}{r} 76 \\ -0 \\ \hline \end{array} \qquad \begin{array}{r} 71 \\ -1 \\ \hline \end{array}$$

$$\begin{array}{r} 77 \\ -4 \\ \hline \end{array} \qquad \begin{array}{r} 74 \\ -3 \\ \hline \end{array} \qquad \begin{array}{r} 80 \\ -4 \\ \hline \end{array} \qquad \begin{array}{r} 72 \\ -1 \\ \hline \end{array}$$

3 Add.

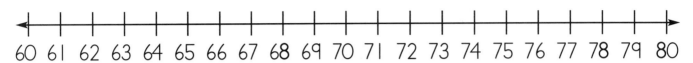

60 61 62 63 64 65 66 67 68 69 70 71 72 73 74 75 76 77 78 79 80

62 + 5 = _____   74 + 3 = _____   68 + 2 = _____

79 + 1 = _____   65 + 4 = _____   73 + 5 = _____

60 + 6 = _____   71 + 7 = _____   64 + 5 = _____

4 Subtract.

10 11 12 13 14 15 16 17 18 19 20

```
  12        14        18        19
-  2      -  3      -  2      -  1
```

```
  15        13        20        11
-  4      -  3      -  6      -  1
```

Horizons Math K Book 2

Lesson 131

---

① Subtract.

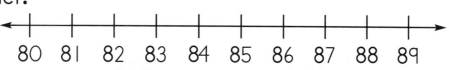

80 81 82 83 84 85 86 87 88 89

```
  87        82        84        85
-  1      -  1      -  3      -  0
```

```
  88        84        89        86
-  2      -  2      -  1      -  2
```

```
  83        87        85        89
-  0      -  2      -  2      -  2
```

---

② Ben has 10¢. Jill gives him 7¢. Altogether, Ben has _____ ¢.

10¢ + 7¢ = _____ ¢

Zach gets 24¢ from his grandfather. Grandma finds another 5¢ for him. Altogether, Zach has _____ ¢.

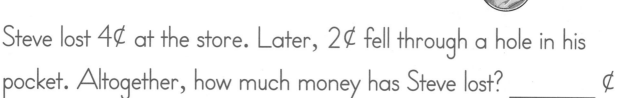

Steve lost 4¢ at the store. Later, 2¢ fell through a hole in his pocket. Altogether, how much money has Steve lost? _____ ¢

3 Add.

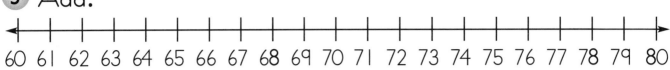

```
  69        74        60        67
+  1      +  5      +  7      +  3
```

```
  61        76        72        63
+  6      +  3      +  4      +  6
```

```
  75        62        65        71
+  4      +  6      +  0      +  5
```

4 Circle the number after.

92	96 95 93	90	91 90 89	95	96 98 93
98	90 99 94	96	91 95 97	93	92 94 96

Lesson 132

1 Write the number before.

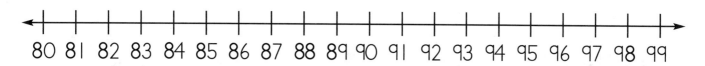

80 81 82 83 84 85 86 87 88 89 90 91 92 93 94 95 96 97 98 99

| _____ 94 | _____ 99 | _____ 93 |

| _____ 95 | _____ 97 | _____ 91 |

| _____ 98 | _____ 96 | _____ 92 |

2 Subtract.

80 – 0 = _____   86 – 3 = _____   83 – 2 = _____

89 – 4 = _____   85 – 5 = _____   88 – 4 = _____

90 – 5 = _____   82 – 1 = _____   87 – 6 = _____

81 – 1 = _____   85 – 0 = _____   86 – 5 = _____

3 Circle . Put an X on  .

4 Match the seasons.

Spring

Fall

Winter

Summer

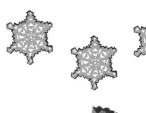

Lesson 133

1 Subtract.

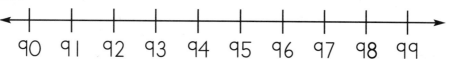

$$90 \quad 91 \quad 92 \quad 93 \quad 94 \quad 95 \quad 96 \quad 97 \quad 98 \quad 99$$

99 – 1 = _____   91 – 1 = _____   95 – 1 = _____

98 – 2 = _____   92 – 2 = _____   94 – 2 = _____

97 – 3 = _____   93 – 0 = _____   93 – 3 = _____

96 – 4 = _____   94 – 1 = _____   92 – 1 = _____

2 Beth has a nickel and 4 pennies. How much money does Beth have altogether? _____ ¢

Nick wants to mail a letter. He buys a stamp for 33¢ and an envelope for 6¢. How much did Nick spend altogether? _____ ¢

Tina buys a gumball for 10¢ and a jawbreaker for 25¢. Altogether, how much did Tina pay for the candy? _____ ¢

© MM, Alpha Omega Publications, Inc.

place value
tens | ones

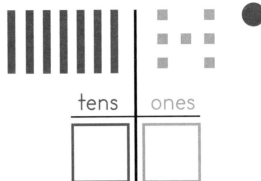

③ Write the numbers.

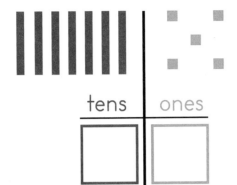

tens | ones

tens | ones

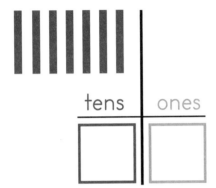

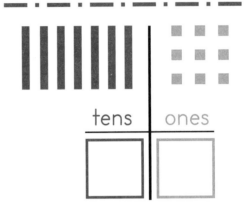

tens | ones

tens | ones

④ Count the money.

   = $ _____

 = $ _____

 = $ _____

 = $ _____

Lesson 134

1 Next door neighbors.

| ____ 2 ____ | ____ 26 ____ |

| ____ 8 ____ | ____ 23 ____ |

| ____ 18 ____ | ____ 4 ____ |

| ____ 12 ____ | ____ 15 ____ |

2 Subtract.

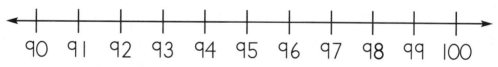

$$\begin{array}{r} 100 \\ -2 \\ \hline \end{array} \qquad \begin{array}{r} 94 \\ -4 \\ \hline \end{array} \qquad \begin{array}{r} 98 \\ -5 \\ \hline \end{array} \qquad \begin{array}{r} 93 \\ -2 \\ \hline \end{array}$$

$$\begin{array}{r} 96 \\ -3 \\ \hline \end{array} \qquad \begin{array}{r} 92 \\ -1 \\ \hline \end{array} \qquad \begin{array}{r} 99 \\ -6 \\ \hline \end{array} \qquad \begin{array}{r} 95 \\ -4 \\ \hline \end{array}$$

3 Bob wrote a poem with 6 sentences. Later he added 2 more sentences. How many sentences are there altogether in the poem? _____

Pat put 6 quarts of oil in the engine of his Nash. The dipstick reads that the engine is one quart low. After Pat adds 1 more quart of oil, how much will he have put in the engine altogether? _____ quarts

4 Count the volumes.

 _____ cups

 _____ liters

 _____ gallons

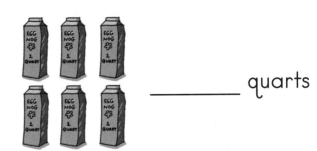 _____ quarts

Horizons Math K Book 2

Lesson 135

1 Write the numbers.

place value

tens | ones

84 = _____ tens and _____ ones.

88 = _____ tens and _____ ones.

_____ = 8 tens and 6 ones.

_____ = 8 tens and 0 ones.

2 The instructions for warming a frozen sandwich are to microwave it for 4 minutes. Then remove the wrapper and microwave it for another 2 minutes. Altogether, how long will the sandwich be in the microwave? _____ minutes

Jan and Drew went hiking. The first trail was 5 miles long and the second trail was 3 miles. How far did they hike altogether on the 2 trails? _____ miles

Horizons Math K Book 2

3 Circle all . Draw a square around the .

4 Count by 5's.

= $ _____

= _____ ¢

= _____ ¢

Horizons Math K Book 2

Lesson 136

1 Subtract.

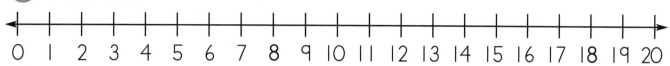

$$6 - 2 = \rule{2cm}{0.4pt} \qquad 12 - 1 = \rule{2cm}{0.4pt} \qquad 7 - 4 = \rule{2cm}{0.4pt}$$

$$9 - 3 = \rule{2cm}{0.4pt} \qquad 15 - 0 = \rule{2cm}{0.4pt} \qquad 16 - 3 = \rule{2cm}{0.4pt}$$

$$20 - 2 = \rule{2cm}{0.4pt} \qquad 11 - 1 = \rule{2cm}{0.4pt} \qquad 4 - 3 = \rule{2cm}{0.4pt}$$

$$6 - 5 = \rule{2cm}{0.4pt} \qquad 18 - 2 = \rule{2cm}{0.4pt} \qquad 12 - 1 = \rule{2cm}{0.4pt}$$

2 Write the numbers.

$$= \rule{2cm}{0.4pt} \cent \qquad\qquad = \rule{2cm}{0.4pt} \cent$$

$$= \$ \rule{2cm}{0.4pt} \qquad\qquad = \$ \rule{2cm}{0.4pt}$$

3 Paul put 24 pens in his desk. One pen did not work.
There were _____ good pens left in Paul's desk.

Marie got 16 cans of soda pop for the party.
Only 4 people at the party had a can of soda.
How many cans of soda were left? _____

There were 8 frogs on a log. 2 went in the water.
How many frogs were left on the log? _____

4 Next door neighbors.

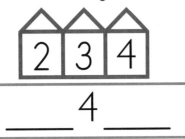

_____ 4 _____

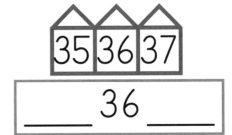

_____ 36 _____

_____ 9 _____

_____ 25 _____

_____ 11 _____

_____ 31 _____

© MM, Alpha Omega Publications, Inc.

Lesson 137

1 Add or subtract.

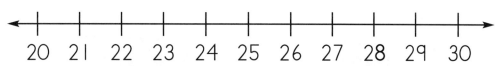

```
  22        27        24        21
+  3      +  2      +  4      +  5
```

```
  26        21        30        24
-  3      -  1      -  3      -  2
```

2 Write the number of items shown on the graph.

_____ cars

_____ bikes

_____ planes

_____ bus

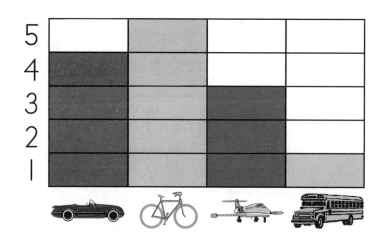

3 Write the missing numbers by 2's.

2   6   8

12   18

22   26

50

4 Circle the largest number in each group.

| 5   9   3 | 6   3   8 |

| 17   15   13 | 17   13   10 |

Lesson 138

place value
tens | ones

1 Write the numbers.

94 = _____ tens and _____ ones.

_____ = 9 tens and 1 one.

_____ = 9 tens and 7 ones.

99 = _____ tens and _____ ones.

2 Count by 4's.

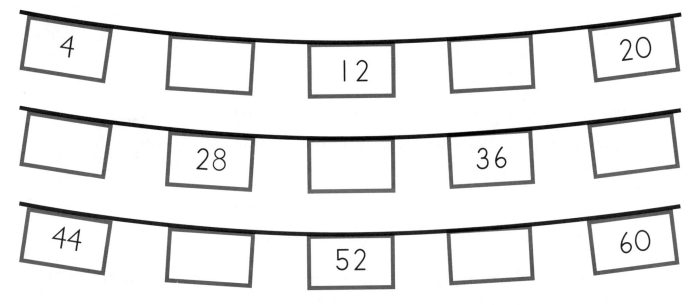

| 4 | | 12 | | 20 |

| | 28 | | 36 | |

| 44 | | 52 | | 60 |

Horizons Math K Book 2

115

3 Subtract.

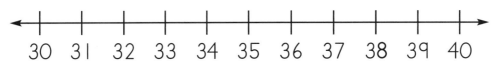

30 31 32 33 34 35 36 37 38 39 40

39 – 4 = _____   35 – 4 = _____   31 – 0 = _____

38 – 5 = _____   32 – 2 = _____   37 – 6 = _____

33 – 0 = _____   40 – 5 = _____   34 – 2 = _____

4 3 boys are in a line. Then 6 more get in line.
How many boys are there altogether in the line?
_____ boys

Judy has 5 big books and 3 little books.
How many books does Judy have altogether?
_____ books

If it takes 10 minutes to do the first page of a lesson
and 5 minutes to do the second page, altogether,
how long will you work on the lesson?
_____ minutes

© MM, Alpha Omega Publications, Inc.

Horizons Math K Book 2

Lesson 139

1 How many centimeters?

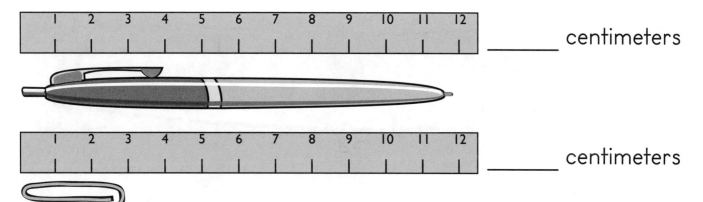

_____ centimeters

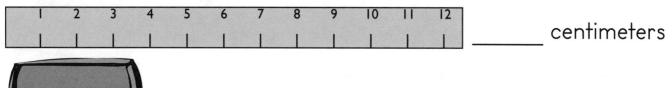

_____ centimeters

_____ centimeters

2 Write the numbers in order.

4	6	3	5
—	—	—	—

3	2	1	4
—	—	—	—

9	7	6	8
—	—	—	—

2	0	1	3
—	—	—	—

3 Count by 3's.

3 6 12 15

21 24

33 39 42

48 54 57

4 Circle the smallest number in each box.

| 6 | 3 | 8 |

| 5 | 9 | 3 |

| 17 | 13 | 10 |

| 17 | 15 | 13 |

| 42 | 39 | 75 |

| 56 | 38 | 79 |

Lesson 140

1 Add or subtract.

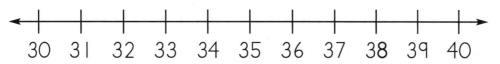

30   31   32   33   34   35   36   37   38   39   40

33 – 2 = _____   39 – 4 = _____   3 4 – 2 = _____

37 – 5 = _____   32 – 1 = _____   36 – 3 = _____

30 + 4 = _____   35 + 4 = _____   31 + 4 = _____

32 + 5 = _____   37 + 3 = _____   34 + 5 = _____

2 Write the numbers in order.

8	6	9	7
—	—	—	—

1	2	4	3
—	—	—	—

5	3	2	4
—	—	—	—

5	4	7	6
—	—	—	—

© MM, Alpha Omega Publications, Inc.

3 6 ducks and 3 ducks are _____ ducks

5 ducks and 5 ducks are _____ ducks

4 ducks and 5 ducks are _____ ducks

7 dogs and 1 dog are _____ dogs

5 dogs and 3 dogs are _____ dogs

8 dogs and 1 dog are _____ dogs

4 Subtract.

```
  50        49        48        47
-  3      -  4      -  5      -  6
```

```
  46        45        44        43
-  1      -  2      -  3      -  0
```

Lesson 141

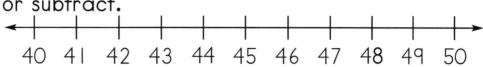

1 Add or subtract.

```
40 41 42 43 44 45 46 47 48 49 50
```

```
  40        41        42        44        45
+  0      +  1      +  2      +  3      +  4
```

```
  46        47        48        49        50
+  3      +  2      +  1      +  0      +  0
```

```
  44        50        42        48        43
-  3      -  5      -  1      -  6      -  2
```

```
  46        41        49        45        47
-  5      -  0      -  6      -  4      -  5
```

2 Write the numbers in order.

```
5   6   4   3          7   6   8   9

__  __  __  __         __  __  __  __
```

3️⃣ These are the winners at the dog show. Match their place in the row with the number for the ribbon.

2nd   5th   1st   3rd   6th   4th

4️⃣ Cross out the number that does not belong when you count by 3's.

3	15 18	24 32
9	17	
6 4	12	30 27
42	60 63	75 83
45	57	
48 52	65	72 78

Lesson 142

① When the big hand on a clock moves one mark, it is a minute. Count the marks by 5's to put the minutes on the outside of the clock.

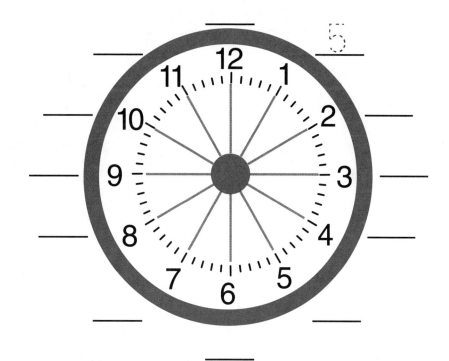

② Cross out the number that does not belong when you count by 4's.

12 8	26 16	32 40
4 9	20 24	34 36
48 44	68 58	72 76
52 41	64 60	78 80

3 Add or subtract.

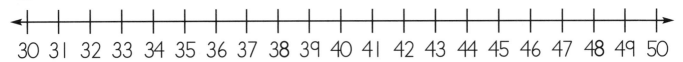

30 31 32 33 34 35 36 37 38 39 40 41 42 43 44 45 46 47 48 49 50

36 + 3 = _____   30 + 5 = _____   40 + 5 = _____

47 + 2 = _____   35 + 4 = _____   41 + 7 = _____

45 + 4 = _____   32 + 6 = _____   38 + 2 = _____

36 – 3 = _____   50 – 5 = _____   40 – 5 = _____

47 – 2 = _____   35 – 4 = _____   48 – 7 = _____

45 – 4 = _____   39 – 6 = _____   38 – 2 = _____

4 Write the numbers.

2 bottles and 4 bottles are _____ bottles.

3 inches and 5 inches are _____ inches.

4 centimeters and 11 centimeters are _____ centimeters.

8 books and 1 book are _____ books.

Lesson 143

① Add or subtract.

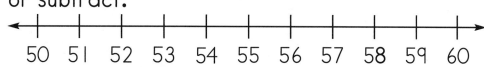

```
  57        54        59        55
-  5      -  3      -  6      -  0
```

```
  50        53        51        58
+  4      +  5      +  2      +  0
```

```
  53        56        58        52
-  2      -  4      -  3      -  1
```

```
  52        55        53        51
+  3      +  4      +  6      +  6
```

② Write the centimeters.

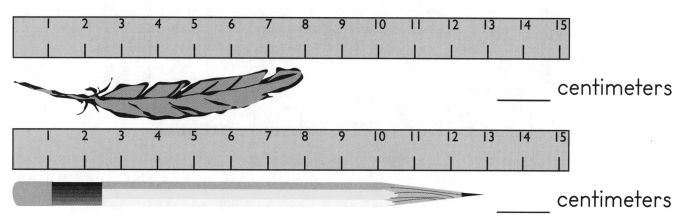

_____ centimeters

_____ centimeters

3 Add.

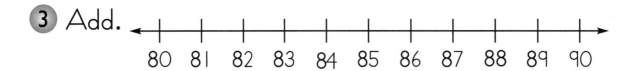

```
  82        86        81        82
+  4      +  3      +  6      +  2
----      ----      ----      ----
```

```
  87        84        83        88
+  1      +  0      +  3      +  1
----      ----      ----      ----
```

4 Find the perimeter.

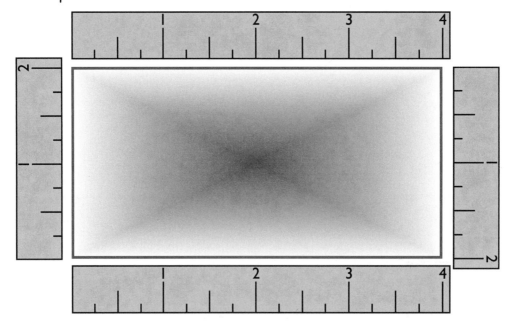

_____ inches

Lesson 144

1 Subtract.

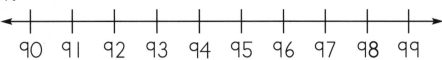

90 91 92 93 94 95 96 97 98 99

94 – 2 = _____   97 – 5 = _____   94 – 0 = _____

93 – 2 = _____   98 – 4 = _____   96 – 3 = _____

95 – 4 = _____   92 – 1 = _____   99 – 6 = _____

2 Put an X on the answers that are wrong.

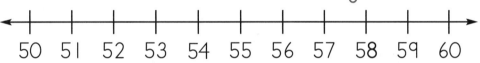

50 51 52 53 54 55 56 57 58 59 60

56 + 3 = 58   52 + 4 = 55   51 + 2 = 52

59 + 0 = 60   53 + 3 = 56   52 + 6 = 58

59 – 3 = 56   52 – 1 = 50   58 – 4 = 54

57 – 2 = 52   55 – 4 = 54   53 – 1 = 52

3 Fran has 28¢. She gives a nickel to Sue. Fran has _____ ¢ left.

April has 3 quarters. She buys a package of gum with 1 quarter. How much money does April have left? _____ ¢

Phil gets $10 for his allowance. On Sunday he will put $1 into his savings. How much money can Phil spend? $ _____

4 Match the addition problems with the correct answer.

| 80 81 82 83 84 85 86 87 88 89 90 |

85 + 4 = _____	86
81 + 3 = _____	83
84 + 2 = _____	88
86 + 2 = _____	87
82 + 5 = _____	89
83 + 0 = _____	84

Lesson 145

1 Add or subtract. Write the letters in the puzzle.

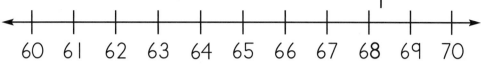

60 61 62 63 64 65 66 67 68 69 70

$62 + 4 =$ _____ a $69 - 1 =$ _____ r

$66 + 3 =$ _____ b $68 - 5 =$ _____ e

$61 + 6 =$ _____ g $64 - 4 =$ _____ o

$62 + 2 =$ _____ j $63 - 2 =$ _____ t

_____ _____ _____ _____ _____   _____ _____ _____ !
67   68   63   66   61   64   60   69

2 Count by 5's to put the minutes around the clock.

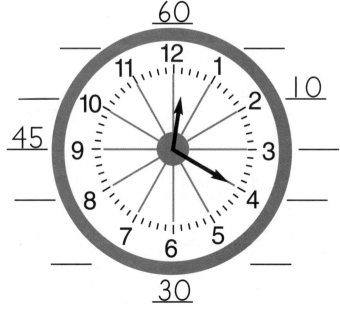

60

____   ____

____   10

45   ____

____   ____

30

What number does the big hand point to?

_____

How many minutes are at the 4? _____

The time is 12:_____

3 Subtract.

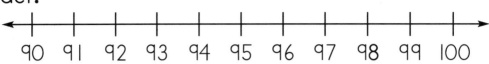

96 − 5	94 − 2	97 − 4	94 − 0	95 − 1

| 98
− 3 | 97
− 2 | 99
− 3 | 98
− 1 | 100
− 2 |

4 Add.

90 + 0	90 + 1	91 + 1	91 + 2

| 90
+ 4 | 92
+ 3 | 94
+ 2 | 96
+ 1 |

| 98
+ 0 | 95
+ 4 | 94
+ 6 |

Lesson 146

1 Write the minutes past the hour.

 2:____

 7:____

 10:____

 4:____

2 Put an X on the wrong answers.

69 − 3 64	65 − 4 61	67 − 3 66	62 − 1 63
68 + 1 69	63 + 4 64	60 + 7 67	62 + 3 65
64 − 4 50	68 − 2 66	63 − 1 72	65 − 4 61

3 Match the geometric solids.

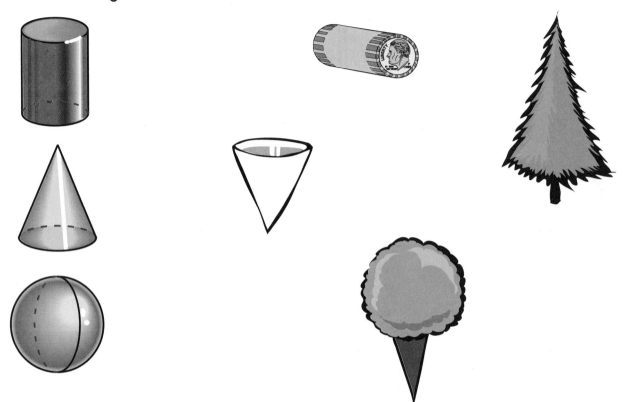

4 Write the number of equal parts.

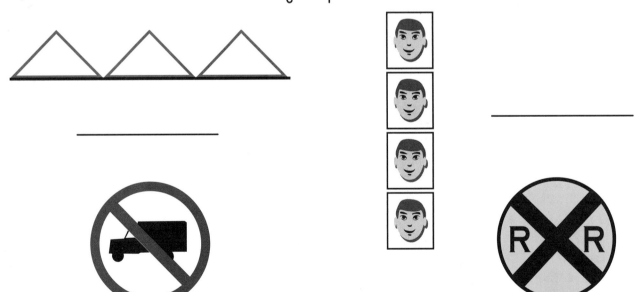

_____   _____

_____   _____

Lesson 147

1 Add or subtract.

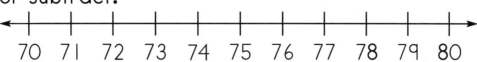

70 71 72 73 74 75 76 77 78 79 80

```
  74          77          70          72
+  4        +  2        +  5        +  3
```

```
  74          77          78          80
-  2        -  4        -  6        -  3
```

2 Match the clocks.

3:05

5:15

8:30

9:50

3 Match the day of the week to the ordinal number.

Sunday   3rd   Thursday

                      7th

Monday   5th

                      1st   Friday

Tuesday   4th

                      2nd

Wednesday   6th   Saturday

4 Add.

$$90 \quad 91 \quad 92 \quad 93 \quad 94 \quad 95 \quad 96 \quad 97 \quad 98 \quad 99 \quad 100$$

$92 + 6 = \underline{}$ m $98 + 1 = \underline{}$ r

$94 + 2 = \underline{}$ b $96 + 1 = \underline{}$ e

$90 + 3 = \underline{}$ n $91 + 4 = \underline{}$ u

Use the letters by the answer to solve the puzzle.

$$\underline{} \quad \underline{} \quad \underline{} \quad \underline{} \quad \underline{} \quad \underline{}$$
$$93 \qquad 95 \qquad 98 \qquad 96 \qquad 97 \qquad 99$$

1

Horizons Math K Book 2

Lesson 148

1 Color the graph for the number of letters used in the sentence.

Ann's cat cannot
eat ants.

	1	2	3	4	5	6
a						
n						
c						
t						
o						
e						
s						

2 Put an X on the wrong answer.

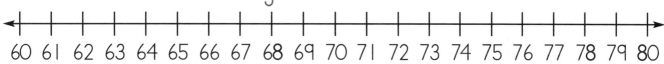

60 61 62 63 64 65 66 67 68 69 70 71 72 73 74 75 76 77 78 79 80

$68 - 5 = 63$ $72 + 3 = 71$ $80 - 4 = 62$

$64 + 1 = 68$ $63 - 1 = 62$ $74 + 3 = 77$

$78 - 6 = 72$ $60 + 7 = 77$ $66 - 3 = 63$

3 Circle the clocks that show half past.

4 Count by 5's to find the number that does not belong.

100	99	25	21	75	85
95	90	35	30	80	79
40	50	65	53	15	19
37	45	60	55	5	10

Lesson 149

1 Add or subtract.

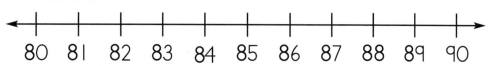

80 81 82 83 84 85 86 87 88 89 90

85 – 2 = _____   83 – 3 = _____   89 – 4 = _____

86 – 5 = _____   84 – 2 = _____   90 – 3 = _____

81 + 4 = _____   87 + 2 = _____   80 + 7 = _____

83 + 0 = _____   88 + 1 = _____   82 + 6 = _____

2 Circle the largest number in each set.

| 25 37 53 | | 17 14 28 |

| 41 35 27 | | 7 10 2 |

| 84 71 62 | | 50 100 75 |

3 Circle the clocks that show a quarter past.

4 Match the money.

© MM, Alpha Omega Publications, Inc.

Lesson 150

place value
tens | ones
⚫ | ⚫

1 Write the numbers.

5 = _____ tens and _____ ones

68 = _____ tens and _____ ones

46 = _____ tens and _____ ones

90 = _____ tens and _____ ones

_____ = 3 tens and 3 ones

_____ = 8 tens and 4 ones

2 Put an X on the wrong answers.

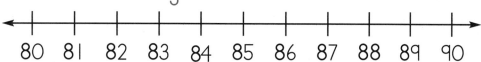

80 81 82 83 84 85 86 87 88 89 90

83	80	89	85
+ 3	+ 2	+ 1	+ 4
89	82	98	89

86	82	87	90
− 5	− 1	− 4	− 2
91	80	83	88

Horizons Math K Book 2

139

© MM, Alpha Omega Publications, Inc.

3 Circle the smallest number in each set.

| 75 | 100 | 50 | | 10 | 2 | 7 | | 14 | 17 | 28 |

| 62 | 71 | 84 | | 35 | 41 | 27 | | 37 | 25 | 53 |

| 0 | 8 | 13 | | 26 | 27 | 25 | | 82 | 61 | 76 |

4 Match the clocks with the same time.

4:50

8:05

9:15

2:20

Horizons Math K Book 2

Lesson 151

1 Write the numbers in order.

| 12 | 11 | 13 | 14 |

___ ___ ___ ___

| 17 | 15 | 16 | 14 |

___ ___ ___ ___

| 16 | 18 | 19 | 17 |

___ ___ ___ ___

| 12 | 11 | 10 | 13 |

___ ___ ___ ___

2 Circle the ordinal numbers.

7th   long   4th

6th

short   one   63

3rd   2nd

92   10th

          two   16

9th

5th   47   1st

8th

big

eleven

3 Write the number before and after.

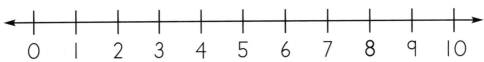

___ 3 ___	___ 7 ___	___ 2 ___
___ 1 ___	___ 5 ___	___ 9 ___
___ 6 ___	___ 4 ___	___ 8 ___

4 Draw a line to match the number to the tally marks.

⊬⊬⊬ 2	⊬⊬⊬ ⊬⊬⊬ 4
// 7	//// 8
⊬⊬⊬ // 5	⊬⊬⊬ /// 10

Lesson 152

1 Add or subtract.

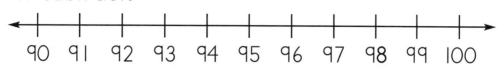

```
  96        91        97        93
+  3      +  4      +  2      +  6
____      ____      ____      ____
```

```
  98        92        95       100
-  3      -  2      -  4      -  5
____      ____      ____      ____
```

2 Write the numbers in order.

```
13   11   14   12
__   __   __   __
```

```
15   14   16   13
__   __   __   __
```

```
17   14   16   15
__   __   __   __
```

```
11   10   13   12
__   __   __   __
```

3 Put an X on the shapes that are not equal parts.

4 Draw a picture for each season.

Summer	Fall
Winter	Spring

Horizons Math K Book 2

© MM, Alpha Omega Publications, Inc.

Lesson 153

1 Write the number between.

3 ____ 5	14 ____ 16	27 ____ 29
35 ____ 37	41 ____ 43	58 ____ 60
62 ____ 64	76 ____ 78	84 ____ 86

2 Put an X on the wrong answers.

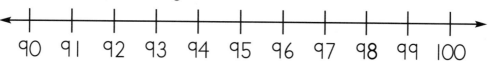

90 91 92 93 94 95 96 97 98 99 100

$$93 - 4 = 99 \qquad 95 - 2 = 93 \qquad 97 - 6 = 95$$

$$90 + 7 = 92 \qquad 96 + 3 = 99 \qquad 94 + 4 = 98$$

$$98 - 3 = 95 \qquad 94 - 4 = 98 \qquad 99 - 4 = 95$$

$$93 + 1 = 92 \qquad 94 + 0 = 94 \qquad 97 + 2 = 100$$

③ Draw hands to show half past.

Draw hands to show quarter past.

④ Write the numbers in order.

18	20	19	17
___	___	___	___

19	16	17	18
___	___	___	___

15	17	18	16
___	___	___	___

16	17	14	15
___	___	___	___

Lesson 154

1 Add or subtract.

8 + 1 = _____   18 + 1 = _____   4 + 3 = _____

6 + 3 = _____   12 + 4 = _____   17 + 2 = _____

8 – 1 = _____   18 – 1 = _____   4 – 3 = _____

6 – 3 = _____   14 – 2 = _____   17 – 2 = _____

2 Write the number between.

| 96 _____ 98 | 87 _____ 89 | 75 _____ 77 |

| 63 _____ 65 | 54 _____ 56 | 42 _____ 44 |

| 38 _____ 40 | 21 _____ 23 | 13 _____ 15 |

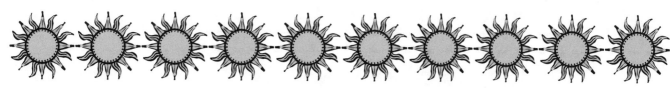

Horizons Math K Book 2

3 Answer the question using the bar graph.

How many dogs? _____

How many cats? _____

How many fish? _____

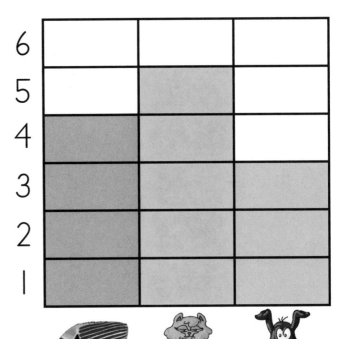

4 Write the numbers in order.

2   3   1   4

___ ___ ___ ___

12   13   11   14

___ ___ ___ ___

19   18   17   16

___ ___ ___ ___

7   6   9   8

___ ___ ___ ___

Lesson 155

1 Add or subtract.

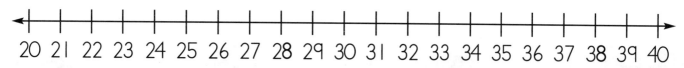

20 21 22 23 24 25 26 27 28 29 30 31 32 33 34 35 36 37 38 39 40

```
  23
+  4
```

```
  36
+  2
```

```
  28
+  2
```

```
  31
+  4
```

```
  27
-  3
```

```
  34
-  4
```

```
  22
-  2
```

```
  39
-  6
```

2 Write the number that comes before and after.

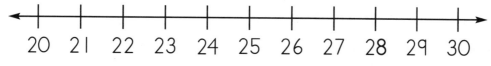

20 21 22 23 24 25 26 27 28 29 30

___ 23 ___	___ 27 ___	___ 22 ___
___ 21 ___	___ 25 ___	___ 29 ___
___ 26 ___	___ 24 ___	___ 28 ___

3 Match the money to the amount.

38¢

$10

75¢

$60

4 Circle the number that is less.

| 6   5 | 2   9 | 2   0 |

| 7   4 | 3   1 | 5   8 |

5 Circle the number that is greater.

| 1   7 | 1   5 | 5   3 |

| 8   0 | 2   3 | 6   8 |

Lesson 156

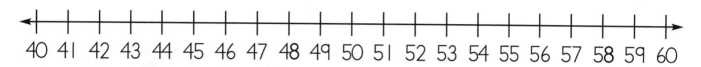

1 Add or subtract.

```
40 41 42 43 44 45 46 47 48 49 50 51 52 53 54 55 56 57 58 59 60
```

46	52	44	58
- 3	- 2	- 0	- 5

42	45	50	54
+ 4	+ 3	+ 4	+ 3

2 Count by 10's to write the number that comes next.

| 10 ____ | 50 ____ | 20 ____ |

| 80 ____ | 60 ____ | 30 ____ |

| 70 ____ | 90 ____ | 40 ____ |

3 Match the geometric solids.

4 Write the numbers on the lines.

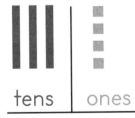

tens	ones

_____ _____

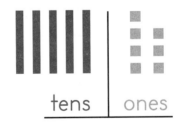

tens	ones

_____ _____

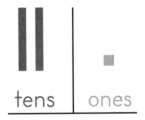

tens	ones

_____ _____

Horizons Math K Book 2

Lesson 157

1 Add or subtract.

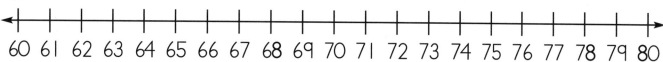

60 61 62 63 64 65 66 67 68 69 70 71 72 73 74 75 76 77 78 79 80

70 + 2 = _____   76 + 3 = _____   60 + 6 = _____

67 + 2 = _____   74 + 5 = _____   61 + 4 = _____

69 + 0 = _____   63 + 4 = _____   72 + 5 = _____

75 – 5 = _____   66 – 3 = _____   69 – 3 = _____

77 – 2 = _____   69 – 5 = _____   72 – 2 = _____

64 – 3 = _____   73 – 3 = _____   65 – 4 = _____

2 Circle the third teddy bear. Put an X on the sixth teddy bear. Put a box around the ninth teddy bear.

3 Count by 5's to write the number after.

5 _____	25 _____	40 _____
70 _____	10 _____	55 _____
35 _____	90 _____	75 _____
15 _____	50 _____	20 _____

4 John has 5 balls. Sal gave him 4 more balls. How many balls does John have altogether?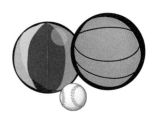

_____

Joe has 3 pears. Dick has 5 pears. How many pears do the boys have altogether?

_____

Horizons Math K Book 2

Lesson 158

1 Add or subtract.

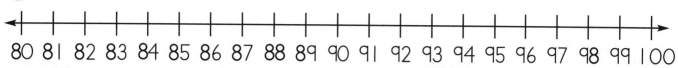

80 81 82 83 84 85 86 87 88 89 90 91 92 93 94 95 96 97 98 99 100

```
  88          82          89          94
-  4        +  3        -  6        +  4
```

```
  97          98          87          85
-  3        +  2        -  5        +  4
```

```
  90          80          86          90
-  2        +  5        -  3        +  4
```

2 Make a tally mark for each object.

3 Write the number.

 _____ cups

 _____ liters

 _____ gallons

 _____ quarts

4 Count by 2's to write the next number.

| 2 _____ | 10 _____ | 24 _____ |

| 6 _____ | 12 _____ | 22 _____ |

| 34 _____ | 46 _____ | 52 _____ |

| 94 _____ | 80 _____ | 76 _____ |

Lesson 159

1 Write in order.

18   17   15   16

___ ___ ___ ___

9   8   10   11

___ ___ ___ ___

2   3   1   0

___ ___ ___ ___

19   17   18   20

___ ___ ___ ___

2 Write the number between.

23 ___ 25	97 ___ 99	61 ___ 63
17 ___ 19	44 ___ 46	50 ___ 52
33 ___ 35	78 ___ 80	66 ___ 68
55 ___ 57	1 ___ 3	82 ___ 84

3 Lisa baked 5 cakes. She gave 1 cake to Rose. How many cakes did Lisa have left?

_____

Bob picked 7 apples. He gave Todd 2 apples. How many apples did Bob have left?

_____

4 Count by 3's to write the next number.

3 ___	15 ___	21 ___
36 ___	42 ___	57 ___
69 ___	78 ___	87 ___
93 ___		

Lesson 160

_ _ _ _ _ _ _ _ _ _ _ _ _ _ _ _ _ _

1 Study the row of cars. Match each with its ordinal number.

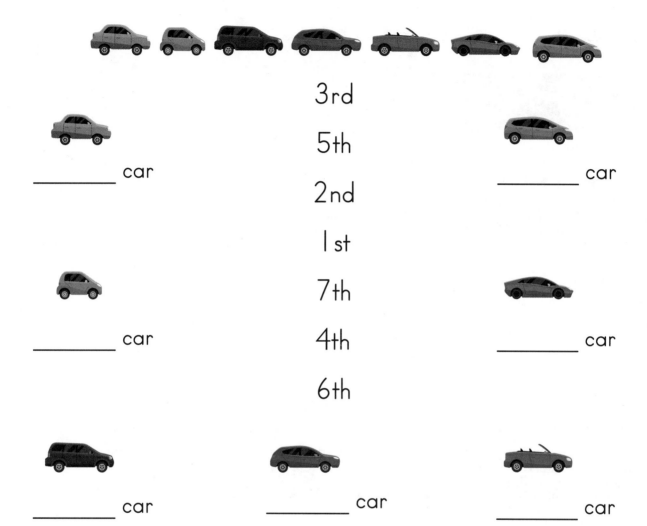

3rd

5th

2nd

1st

7th

4th

6th

_____ car   _____ car

_____ car   _____ car

_____ car   _____ car   _____ car

2 Count by 4's to write the next number.

4 _____	12 _____	16 _____	24 _____
32 _____	44 _____	56 _____	64 _____
76 _____	88 _____	80 _____	96 _____

Horizons Math K Book 2

3 Write the number.

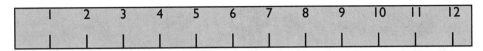

_____ centimeters

_____ centimeters

_____ centimeters

4 Write the number.

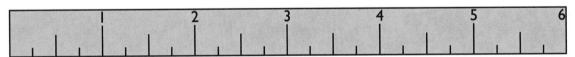

_____ inches

_____ inches

_____ inches